JANE EYRE

PORTRAIT
OF A LIFE

TWAYNE'S MASTERWORK STUDIES

Robert Lecker, General Editor

JANE EYRE

PORTRAIT
OF A LIFE

Maggie Berg

TWAYNE PUBLISHERS • BOSTON
A Division of G.K. Hall & Co.

Jane Eyre: Portrait of a Life
Maggie Berg

Twayne's Masterwork Studies No. 10

Copyright 1987 by G.K. Hall & Co.
All rights reserved.
Published by Twayne Publishers
A Division of G.K. Hall & Co.
70 Lincoln Street
Boston, Massachusetts 02111

Copyediting supervised by Lewis DeSimone
Book production by Janet Zietowski

Typeset in 10/14 Sabon with Optima display type
by Compset, Inc., of Beverly, Massachusetts

Printed on permanent/durable acid-free paper
and bound in the United States of America

Library of Congress Cataloging in Publication Data

Berg, Maggie.
  Jane Eyre : portrait of a life

  (Twayne's masterwork studies ; no. 10)
  Bibliography: p.
  Includes index.
  1. Brontë, Charlotte, 1816–1855. Jane Eyre.
  2. Fiction, Autobiographic—History and criticism.
  I. Title. II. Series.
✓PR4167.J5B4 1987   823'.8   87-14877
  ISBN 0-8057-7955-8 (alk. paper)
  ISBN 0-8057-8010-6 (pbk. : alk. paper)

This book is for Mater.

CONTENTS

NOTE ON REFERENCES AND ACKNOWLEDGMENTS

All references in the text are to the Penguin Books paperback edition of *Jane Eyre* (1985), with its excellent introduction and notes by Q. D. Leavis.

The quotation from Robert Browning's "Fra Lippo Lippi" on page 34, is reprinted by permission of Oxford University Press from *The Poetical Works of Robert Browning*, edited by Ian Jack (Oxford University Press, 1970).

I wish to thank Robert Lecker for his intelligent and exacting assistance; also Mary Stinson, Richard Hamilton, Lallie Grauer, Peter O'Brien, Barbara Leckie, John Berg, Anthony Suter, Genevieve Gilchrist, Peggy Rice, Tony Crowle, and Jackie Grant; but above all I am grateful to the students in my first class at McGill whose enthusiasm prompted me to write this book.

Charlotte Brontë
Portrait by G. Richmond
Courtesy of the National Portrait Gallery, London

CHRONOLOGY: CHARLOTTE BRONTË'S LIFE AND WORKS

1812	29 December, the Reverend Patrick Brontë marries Maria Branwell.
1814	Maria born in April.
1815	Rev. Patrick Brontë publishes *The Cottage in the Wood; or, The Art of Becoming Rich and Happy*. Elizabeth born in February. 19 May, family moves to St. James' Church, Thornton.
1816	21 April, Charlotte Brontë born; christened 29 June.
1817	26 June, Patrick Branwell Brontë born.
1818	Rev. Patrick Brontë publishes *The Maid of Killarney; or Albion and Marina: A Modern Tale* and 2d ed. of *The Cottage in the Wood*. In February Maria Brontë (Charlotte's mother) is ill. In July Emily Jane Brontë born.
1820	17 January, Anne Brontë born. Rev. Brontë receives stipend for curacy at Howarth; family moves in April.
1821	Aunt Branwell comes to care for her sister and the children in January. In February Charlotte's mother is very ill. On 15 September Maria Branwell dies, probably of cancer.
1824	Maria and Elizabeth go to the clergy daughters' school at Cowan Bridge in July. Charlotte joins her sisters in August, and in November Emily is also there.
1825	In February, Maria sent home very ill; she dies in May. In May, Elizabeth also very ill; she dies in June. Charlotte and Emily taken away from the school.
1826	In June the children begin their "great plays" or games with Branwell's toy soldiers, which they chronicle at great length in various forms.
1829	Charlotte has produced, according to her own estimate, "22 volumes" of tales, poetry, etc.

1831	Charlotte, fourteen years old, enrolls in Miss Wooler's school at Roe Head (between Leeds and Huttersfield), where she meets her lifelong friends Ellen Nussey and Mary Taylor.
1832	Charlotte returns home in May to tutor her sisters and take drawing lessons. Writes, with Patrick, the "Angrian" stories, while Emily and Anne write the "Gondal" saga.
1835	Charlotte goes back as a teacher to Roe Head in July, and Emily joins her as a pupil, but is homesick and leaves in October; Anne comes the following year.
1836	At home for Christmas, the sisters discuss writing for money. Charlotte sends poems to Southey (poet laureate) in December; receives a discouraging reply.
1838	Anne unwell at Roe Head School; Charlotte reproaches Miss Wooler and resigns her post.
1839	Charlotte's first post as a governess with the Sidgewicks near Skipton; finds it an ordeal and returns home.
1840	Charlotte at home writing during her spare time and reading extensively, including French novels.
1841	Charlotte a governess (for the last time) until December, when she recognizes "how utterly averse" she is to it.
1842	Charlotte and Emily go to Brussels in February, to study at the Pensionnat Heger. Despite their overdemanding professor, M. Heger, Charlotte is never unhappy. In November they return home because Aunt Branwell is very ill, but she dies before they arrive.
1843	Charlotte returns alone to Brussels in January but becomes homesick and hopelessly in love with M. Heger.
1844	Charlotte returns home, using her father's blindness as an excuse. Extremely depressed by the situation with M. Heger, is "tamed down and broken." Charlotte, Emily, and Anne make detailed plans for establishing a school, but "there are no pupils to be had."
1845	Branwell, dismissed from his tutorship, is at home, depressed and alcoholic. Charlotte is pining for M. Heger. The sisters discover that each writes poetry, and they plan a small publication under the acronyms of Currer, Ellis, and Acton Bell.
1846	*Poems: by Currer, Ellis and Acton Bell*, published in May. Charlotte finishes *The Professor* (her first novel), but it is refused by the publishers; she begins *Jane Eyre*. Emily writes *Wuthering Heights* and Anne, *Agnes Grey*.

Chronology

1847   *Agnes Grey* and *Wuthering Heights* published by Thomas Newby in December. *The Professor* rejected by Smith, Elder & Co. in August; but encouraged by their criticisms of it, Charlotte sends *Jane Eyre,* which is accepted and published six weeks later on 16 October. Charlotte tells her father for the first time that she has written a book. In November Charlotte begins a lasting correspondence with George Lewes (later husband of George Eliot).

1848   Second edition of *Jane Eyre* in January, dedicated to Thackeray, which causes gossip that the author was Thackeray's governess (Thackeray's wife was insane). Charlotte denies, even to her closest friend, Ellen Nussey, that she has published a novel. In July, the sisters receive news from Smith, Elder & Co. that *Jane Eyre, Wuthering Heights,* and *Agnes Grey* are being offered to American houses, as the work of a single author. Charlotte and Anne go to London to prove their separate identities; it becomes certain that Currer, Ellis, and Acton Bell are women. Later that summer Anne's *The Tenant of Wildfell Hall* published by T. C. Newby. Branwell dies in September; Charlotte ill because of it. In November Emily very ill, but refuses medical aid, and dies in December (immediately after agreeing to see a doctor). Anne is also very ill.

1849   Anne dies while at Scarborough in May. Charlotte is desolate and alone, except for her father. Is kept going by writing *Shirley,* which she completes in September. In November Charlotte goes to London (which she was always afraid of) and meets her idol, Thackeray, and Harriet Martineau.

1850   In January she is extremely upset by George Lewes's sexist review of *Shirley* but in June visits London again and meets Lewes himself, who looks so much like Emily that she says she cannot hate him. In August meets Elizabeth Gaskell; they soon become friends. In September Charlotte writes a preface to the memorial edition of *Agnes Grey* and *Wuthering Heights.*

1851   Charlotte horrified by her friend Harriet Martineau's *Letters on the Laws of Man's Nature and Development,* just published. Visits London in May to attend Thackeray's lectures and see the Great Exhibition. Visits Mrs. Gaskell in Birmingham (again in April 1853 and May 1854).

1852   In December the Reverend Arthur Nicolls, who had been curate at Howarth since 1845, unexpectedly proposes marriage. Charlotte immediately tells her father, who is so distressed that she promises to refuse. Rev. Nicolls resigns his post and leaves.

1853   *Villette* published. Mrs. Gaskell's *Ruth* also published.

1854   Rev. Brontë allows Rev. Nicolls to return to the curacy at Howarth; Charlotte and he become engaged.

1854   Charlotte Brontë marries Rev. Arthur Nicolls on 29 June; she is very happy with her "dear husband."

1855   Charlotte, believed pregnant, suffers from acute and unremitting nausea. 31 March, Charlotte Brontë dies.

1857   Elizabeth Gaskell's *The Life of Charlotte Brontë* is published in March with a preface by Arthur Nicolls.

— 1 —

HISTORICAL CONTEXT

When *Jane Eyre* came out in 1847 it so accurately reflected contemporary life that it was assumed to be the true story of "an oppressed orphan, a starved and bullied charity-school girl, and a despised and slighted governess."[1] It appeared in the decade known as the "Hungry Forties" in which the oppression and poverty of Jane's youth were the common experience of England's working population.[2] Deprivation is, however, only half the story. Jane also achieves education, financial independence, and social status; through her own effort and will she transforms her life. But more important than Jane's altered material circumstances is the fundamental state of existence that they reflect. The Victorians, like Jane, were searching in an unstable and uncertain world for a new identity, and they too needed "courage to go forth into its expanse."[3] Jane's evolving and ambiguous state is conveyed through an appropriately evolving and ambiguous literary mode. Until the conclusion of the autobiography Jane is outwardly an anomaly and inwardly divided. Jane's crises are caused by constant radical changes: in this respect her story embodies a time of social transformation. In both subject and style *Jane Eyre* illustrates the conflicts of an age in a state of transition. We shall see that Charlotte Brontë had artistic, as well as political, reasons for making her heroine an orphan, a governess, and, finally, a writer.

Nothing better exemplifies the paradoxes of Victorian society than Jane's first profession: The governess, of which there were 25,000 in 1851, was a product of social transformations caused by the Industrial Revolution. Although she was hired as a status symbol by new middle-class families to teach their children, a governess was in fact little more than a domestic, working long hours for almost no money.[4] She was usually from a more genteel family than the one she worked for, but her poverty and superior education made her an object of suspicion and resentment on all sides: she was "above" the servants and "below" the employers. Brontë felt that "a private governess has no existence, is not considered as a living and rational being except as connected with the wearisome duties she has to fulfil."[5] Perhaps because of the rigid routine and the loneliness, ex-governesses were, as Brontë's friend Harriet Martineau discovered, the largest group of women in Victorian mental asylums.[6] It seems that the raving Bertha Mason shut up in Thornfield Hall was the shadow hanging over every Victorian governess. Brontë's frustration as a governess frequently made her ill, but perhaps the writing of *Jane Eyre,* which was her own affirmation of a private existence, saved her from a similar fate.

Jane Eyre rises above her terrible oppression through her own willpower; her life illustrates the extremely popular Victorian notion of "Self-Help." Samuel Smiles's book of that name, offering social success through hard work, was the best-selling book of Brontë's time, outstripping all works of fiction.[7] Brontë's own father was an exemplary "self-made man" who had been born an Irish peasant but had educated himself sufficiently to obtain a degree in theology from Cambridge. In 1811 he published *The Cottage in the Wood; or, The Art of Becoming Rich and Happy,* whose moral is in its title. *Jane Eyre* describes how a woman may become "rich and happy" through patient self-advancement. The individualistic ethic in *Jane Eyre* is partly an expression of the contemporary popularizing of the philosophies of Jeremy Bentham and John Stuart Mill, but it is more directly due to the influence of Brontë's father. Perhaps inspired by the Christian belief that all are equal in the sight of God, the Reverend Brontë gave his daughters an intellectual education; rather than the "ornamental" education that was customary for women (consisting of reading, music, sewing, and drawing), and even discussed with them the "male" subject of politics. When Jane Eyre makes what was considered an unfeminine declaration of equality with Rochester it is on the basis of their Christian souls (281).

But Brontë's religious upbringing was contradictory. Her mother once wrote a tract whose title contrasts strikingly with her husband's work. "The Advantages of Poverty in Religious Concerns" suggests an acquiescence in one's lot that is as much symptomatic of being a woman as a Christian at that time. Many women rationalized and even glorified their lives of deprivation and inferiority with the Christian principle of self-denial. When Brontë read Harriet Taylor Mill's objection to the oppression of women in 1851 (which anticipated her husband J. S. Mill's more famous *The Subjection of Women* [1869]), she said that the writer had a "hard jealous heart" and "forgets there is such a thing as self-sacrificing love and disinterested devotion."[8]

Brontë was not, then, a "Strong-Minded Woman," the pejorative name given to the forerunners of feminism who were demanding higher education, a parliamentary vote, and increased employment for women, but she was nevertheless concerned with the "Woman Question" or the role of women in society. She was therefore drawn to other leading women writers of her time. Elizabeth Gaskell, later Brontë's official biographer, became her closest friend, perhaps because both were successful novelists writing about contemporary social problems. Brontë's *Shirley* (1842) is similar to Gaskell's *North and South* (1855), except that Brontë's depiction of the Luddite riots in which men attacked cotton mills in the north of England because of famine was less sympathetic to the working class than was Gaskell's work. *Ruth* (1853) is Gaskell's story of an orphan; it depicts the terrible working conditions of a seamstress (in 1847 a Parliamentary Act endeavored to *limit* the average working day to ten hours). Ruth was a fallen woman who went on to lead a saintly life. Brontë admired the theme, but objected to Mrs. Gaskell's "slaying of the victim" (L, 475). It seems she wanted images of successful women. Brontë's other close friend in her mature years (until they disagreed over *Jane Eyre*) was Harriet Martineau, one of the leading social critics, historians, and feminists of the age. Although Brontë almost never agreed with Martineau's views, she considered her life to be great, noble, and "exemplary" (L, 439).

Martineau's atheism, however, aroused in Brontë "instinctive horror." Her *Letters on the Laws of Man's Nature and Development* (1851) was, said Brontë, "the first unequivocal declaration of disbelief in the existence of God or a future life I have ever seen" (L, 441). Brontë felt that if Martineau's views were true, life was insupportable. Like most of her contemporaries, she resisted the implications of Darwin's *The Origin of Species* (1832), declaring, in words that echo Tennyson, that it was impossible to "rejoice over this hopeless blank" (L, 441). In her youth Brontë, like many of her notable contemporaries (John Stuart Mill, Thomas Carlyle, Henry Newman), experienced a religious crisis that is dramatized in *Villette* (1853) when the heroine, who hates Roman Catholicism, nevertheless goes to confession to relieve her spiritual torments. Influenced by her aunt's Calvinism, Brontë was afraid that she might be damned because of her uncontrollable fantasies.[9] Although she tried to stop writing, she clung tenaciously to her religion. In her inability to contemplate a mechanical universe Brontë was typical of her time. When Jane Eyre is wandering on the heath totally abandoned (God the Father is very far away and Mother Nature barely supports her) and in search of whatever would make life tolerable, she clearly represents a fundamental Victorian state.

While Jane's orphaned and outcast condition represented a spiritual truth about the Victorian state of existence it also signified an artistic truth for Brontë, who explained to Wordsworth the joy she felt in creating characters with "no father nor mother but your own imagination" (L, 201). Jane Eyre was indeed created in defiance of the tradition of heroines: Brontë wanted her to have no literary ancestors.[10] Elizabeth Barrett Browning similarly made her fictional artist *Aurora Leigh* (1857) an orphan, to symbolize her own lament that women writers in the nineteenth century had no "grandmothers," by which

she meant a female literary tradition.[11] If Jane's lack of a family, however, prompts her search for identity and gives her the freedom to look
for it, the same can be said of Brontë's literary ancestry.

Brontë was searching beyond what she called "the jargon of Conventionality" for her own "language of Truth,"[12] but because of the
time in which she wrote she was torn. She was extremely influenced
by the previous generation of romantic poets; from the age of six she
wrote hundreds of stories of love and adventure featuring Byronic
heroes like Rochester, and in her adolescence she sent work to Wordsworth, Robert Southey, Hartley Coleridge, and de Quincey. Brontë's
early inclination to fantasize is expressed in *Jane Eyre* as the romantic
belief in the power of the individual imagination to animate and therefore confer meaning on the external world: Brontë believed with Samuel Taylor Coleridge that "I may not hope from outward forms to win
the passion and the life, whose fountains are within."[13] But this belief
in the value of subjectivity was counteracted by Brontë's acute awareness of what George Eliot called "the high responsibilities of literature
that undertakes to represent life,"[14] and she shared with her contemporaries the belief that in order to "criticise life" she had to present it
objectively. The Victorian reading public was, moreover, losing its
taste for the romantic tales of Walter Scott and the Gothic excitement
of Walpole and was demanding the domestic novel, describing the
lives of men and women like themselves. Just as large an audience
looked forward to the penny public readings of Charles Dickens's novels as await the soap operas on television today; and fictional characters became popular heroes and heroines: Thackeray's Becky Sharp
in *Vanity Fair*[15] vied with Jane for public favor, and Rochester inspired
a cult of truculent and brooding lovers. Brontë believed that this realistic reception of fiction could be very useful and called William
Thackeray "the first social regenerator of the day" (36).

In *Jane Eyre* Brontë searches for a reconciliation between her conflicting romantic and realistic aspirations. Something similar was hap-
pening in the world of painting: in 1847, the year that *Jane Eyre* was
published, a group of young painters known as the Pre-Raphaelites
banded together in opposition to the conventional teachings of the

time and agreed that art should "return to Nature," but they used detailed realistic description for symbolic purposes, in order to convey a hidden emotional reality. John Ruskin, the art critic who identified with the aims of the Pre-Raphaelites, advocated in *Modern Painters* (the first two volumes of which had appeared in 1841 and 1846) an imaginative apprehension of the world that reconciled subjectivity with imitation. Brontë admired Ruskin very much, calling him "one of the few genuine writers, as distinguished from book-makers, of this age" (L, 442).

Many would say the same of Brontë. In order to convey the psychological undercurrents of everyday reality, she effectively created a new literary genre, which Robert Heilman[16] called "New Gothic" but which could more appropriately be called "domestic Gothic." In *Jane Eyre* Brontë reconciled the demands of her social conscience, which required her to be realistic, with her celebration of the individual imagination, which explained her natural tendency to romanticism. While the oppressive circumstances of Jane's life reflect the social conditions of the mid-nineteenth century, the power with which she overcomes them is essentially a romantic conception. It is Jane's imagination that pushes her on to greater things, and it is her belief in herself that carries her up the steep "Path of advance"[17] (as Matthew Arnold called it). This is perhaps why the Victorians believed that Jane was a real person. When reviewers criticized Jane's morality, they did so because they feared her; and while they attacked *Jane Eyre*, the Victorian public continued to read it avidly.

– 2 –

THE IMPORTANCE OF THE WORK

It is the reading public that establishes the popularity of a novel, however much critics may discuss the concept of "greatness," and *Jane Eyre* is undeniably one of the most popular of English novels. While reviewers were debating its merits, Victorian readers couldn't put it down, and it soon acquired a cult following.[18] Thackeray, who received a complementary copy, said it made him cry; he "lost . . . a whole day in reading it at the busiest period" (CH, 70). It is private remarks such as this that most clearly attest to the impact of a work. Lady Cavendish confided to her journal that *Jane Eyre* was

> the most powerful novel I ever read; the authoress turns oneself and one's opinions round her thumb. I thought my principles were pretty well established with regard to bigamy, but I could have been heard at the moment fervently wishing that circumstances had kept Jane ignorant of the first wife's existence. N.B. I repented afterwards.[19]

What is interesting about this comment is the fact that the emotional effect of *Jane Eyre* was, as the reviewers feared, sufficiently strong enough to undermine long-standing prejudices. While a good novel may move us, only an excellent one can significantly alter our ideas. In 1855 Mrs. Oliphant, herself a successful Victorian novelist, looked back on the unsettling effect of *Jane Eyre*, attributing to it nothing less than a social and literary "revolution": "Ten years ago we professed an orthodox system of novel-making. Our lovers were humble and devoted. . . . when suddenly there stole upon the scene . . . a dangerous little person . . . , and the most alarming revolution of modern times has followed the invasion of *Jane Eyre*" (CH, 311–12).

The effect of *Jane Eyre* reaches far beyond the interest, or even the emotional content, of the narrative. Brontë "invaded" personal and literary spheres simultaneously because they are, as Mrs. Oliphant recognised, interconnected in the novel. Brontë wished to explore the protagonist's inner life without ignoring the importance of everyday existence, and in order to do so she effectively created a new genre that, Robert Heilman argues, extends areas of human experience hitherto created in the novel.[20] Brontë invested an ostensibly realistic narrative with the ideals of romanticism inherited from her predecessors, but in doing so she created much more than a combination of genres. *Jane Eyre* is regarded as transitional (and therefore of pivotal importance) because, as Sandra Gilbert and Susan Gubar say, it "summarizes influential earlier traditions and at the same time forecasts crucial later developments in those traditions."[21] But to call *Jane Eyre* either a summary or a forecast is to miss a dimension in it that is unique and unrelated to Brontë's position in literary history. By "tradition," Gilbert and Gubar mean that *Jane Eyre* (along with two other much shorter novellas) was considered worth anthologizing in full because the "plots, themes, and images have been especially important in delineating the distinctively female literary tradition that our anthology charts."[22]

Like other works of lasting importance, *Jane Eyre*, with its multiplicity of meaning, provides fertile ground for analysis. This is perhaps because the subject—an individual search for identity—inevitably raises issues of abiding importance: the injustices of poverty and the difficulties of rising above it; the need to establish one's own beliefs in contradistinction to the dictates of church and society; and the necessity of reconciling the often contradictory needs for love and independence.

While the narrative of Jane's quest engages our attention and elicits our sympathy, something else is achieved by the text, something more fundamental that takes place beneath the surface, which critics continue to attempt to define.[23] Attention to the pattern of imagery in *Jane Eyre* indicates Brontë's pre-Freudian understanding of how our unacknowledged emotions reveal themselves and of how our unconscious wishes affect our everyday lives. It was perhaps this subliminal aspect in *Jane Eyre* that prompted Lady Cavendish to "fervently" wish that Jane had unknowingly committed bigamy.

The "powerful" effect of *Jane Eyre* on its readers may be due to its perennial subject, the continuing importance of its social and philosophical content, or its underlying passion. This would certainly be enough to make it a best-seller, but it doesn't explain Mrs. Oliphant's claim that *Jane Eyre* also influenced writers and their ideas about the novel. The purely literary impact of *Jane Eyre* has been very belatedly understood: only in the past ten to fifteen years have critics begun to appreciate what Mrs. Oliphant called Brontë's "system of novel-making," or the language, structure, and style of *Jane Eyre*; and only very recently has it been treated as self-contained discourse independent of its author.[24]

But what gives *Jane Eyre* its purely literary importance is that while the reader is involved in Jane's changing fortunes and emotions, Brontë is using the exploration of an individual psyche to examine how that psyche affects artistic vision. Jane is herself an artist, and the narrator of the autobiography, so that her changing perspective alters the manner and style of telling the story. While Jane is engaged in discovering her personal convictions, the narrator (also Jane) is exploring artistic ones: Jane's search for herself parallels the mature autobiographer's search for an artistic identity. *Jane Eyre* is, as Mrs. Oliphant recognised, as important in aesthetic as in social terms because apart from being a fascinating and moving story, it also offers an analysis of itself as a work of art. This aspect of the novel has been overlooked.

— 3 —

CRITICAL RECEPTION

The history of the criticism of *Jane Eyre* reveals how influential and perhaps detrimental can be the early reactions to a novel. Although critical attitudes and assumptions have radically altered in the past hundred years, critics today are still answering questions raised by the reviewers in 1849 and 1850.

In the mid-nineteenth century critics were concerned above all with whether a novel was true to life, and then with the effect it would have on its readers' morality. While all early reviews considered *Jane Eyre* to be vividly realistic, not all agreed that this placed it in "the exalted region of art" (CH, 85), as one critic put it. Brontë's contemporaries were hotly divided over whether *Jane Eyre* was spiritually uplifting and morally conformist, or dangerously subversive and immoral. Although twentieth-century critics are concerned with neither the accuracy nor the morality of *Jane Eyre*, they are still interested in why the book provoked such a divided first reaction, and they search for their answer in the text itself. If the critical ground has shifted since *Jane Eyre*'s appearance, from a thematic to a stylistic emphasis, the purpose seems to have remained to explain what Mary Jacobus recently called the "secretive, unstable and subversive"[25] undercurrents in Brontë's writing.

Critical Reception

"Lose not a day in sending for it" (CH, 84), said George Lewes in one of the first reviews of *Jane Eyre*. The "great characteristic" that distinguished this new novel from the "trashy" romances of the time was, noted Lewes, "Reality—deep, significant reality" (CH, 84). Because *Jane Eyre* offered "transcripts from the book of life" that were "breathing flesh and blood" (CH, 85), it was hailed by another critic as "an omen of good. It indicates a departure from the sickly models of the Minerva Press [a publishing house for popular women's novels]" (CH, 81). The word "model" is revealing: fictional characters were regarded, in the nineteenth century, as moral examplars, so that if a book were, like *Jane Eyre,* primarily about women, reviewers became anxious over the effect it might have on the behavior of the impressionable "fair sex." A year after the publication of *Jane Eyre,* Elizabeth Rigby expressed concern that the sales of the book were so high:

> Mr. Rochester is a man who deliberately and secretly seeks to violate the laws both of God and man, and yet we will be bound half our lady readers are enchanted with him for a model of generosity and honour. We would have thought that such a hero had had no chance, in the purer taste of the present day; but the popularity of *Jane Eyre* is a proof how deeply the love of the illegitimate romance is implanted in our nature. (CH, 107)

The Victorians were in a double bind: they wanted truth, but too much of it could be disturbing; their demand for realism was frequently at odds with their need for spiritual elevation. The problem with *Jane Eyre,* said one reviewer, was that its very credibility made repeated "assaults upon the prejudices of proper people" (CH, 99). Jane Eyre's temptation to transgress "the laws of God and man" and stay with Rochester was so vividly presented that it threatened the reader's complacency. While one supporter claimed that the "obvious moral" of *Jane Eyre* was that "laws, both human and divine, approved in our calmer moments, are not to be disobeyed when our time of trial comes" (CH, 79), not all were convinced about the value of Jane's "daring peep into regions which acknowledge the authority of no conventional rules" (CH, 99).

Victorian critics would satisfy themselves about the morality of a literary work by inquiring into the moral credentials of its author. *Jane Eyre* was surely based on real experience, but whose? When the book came out under the male pseudonym of Currer Bell, its author was respected for his championship of "the weaker party," and the vigorous style was praised:

> There can be no question but that *Jane Eyre* is a very clever book. Indeed it is a book of decided power. The thoughts are true, sound, and original; and the style, though rude and uncultivated here and there, is resolute, straightforward, and to the purpose. . . . the object and moral of the work is excellent. (CH, 76)

The authorship, however, was quickly doubted: "who," asked one anonymous reviewer, "but a woman, could have ventured . . . to fill three octavo volumes with the history of a woman's heart?" (CH, 89). The search for evidence of the author's sex led to such observations as: "no woman trusses game and garnishes dessert-dishes with the same hands" and "No lady . . . when suddenly roused in the night, would think of hurrying on 'a frock' "; but these profundities were meant to show that *Jane Eyre* was probably written by a woman "who has, for some sufficient reason, long forfeited the society of her own sex" (CH, 111).

Charlotte Brontë later explained that she and her sisters had chosen to write under male pseudonyms because they had the "impression" that "authoresses are liable to be looked on with prejudice; we noticed how critics sometimes use for their chastisement the weapon of personality, and for their reward, a flattery, which is not true praise." (L, 286). Little did the Brontës expect that the very subjective criticism they feared would be exacerbated by speculation. "Come what will," said Charlotte Brontë, "I cannot, when I write, think always of myself and of what is elegant and charming in feminity" (L, 386). Although the sisters had not in the least supposed "that our mode of writing and thinking was not what is called 'feminine,' " they were quickly accused, when believed to be women, of "masculine" style. The very characteristics that were admired when the book was assumed to be written by a man, condemned it when it was thought to be by a woman. George Lewes, who had been one of Brontë's strongest supporters, despite knowing her sex, now wrote that the "vigour often amounts to coarseness,—and is certainly the very antipode to 'lady like' " (CH, 163).

Most reviews mingled praise with blame: (such virile style and moral frankness were inexcusable in a woman.) The equanimity with which Jane listens to Rochester's revelations was considered "revolting and improbable" (CH, 114), while "the profanity, brutality, and slang of the misanthropic profligate" himself were "torpedo shocks to the nervous system" (CH, 98). This same critic for the *North American Review* paid Brontë the tribute of creating a "mental epidemic, passing under the name of 'Jane Eyre fever' " (CH, 97), in which "that portion of Young America known as ladies' men began to swagger and swear in the presence of the gentler sex, and to allude darkly to events in their lives which excused impudence and profanity" (CH, 97–98). The popularity of *Jane Eyre* was, he concluded, "due in part to the freshness, raciness, and vigor of mind it evinced" (CH, 99). It was these qualities that produced such deeply ambivalent reactions as that of the male critic who inadvertently condemned himself:

> A book more unfeminine, both in its excellences and defects, it would be hard to find in the annals of female authorship. Throughout there is masculine power, breadth and shrewdness, combined with masculine hardness, coarseness, and freedom of expression. (CH, 89)

The author of *Jane Eyre,* concluded Elizabeth Rigby and others, must be a women "unsexed."[26] Charlotte Brontë asked her feminist friend Harriet Martineau whether she thought there were any truth in the remark, and she replied that *Jane Eyre* merely treated love more openly than was customary. Martineau later accused Brontë of being too typically feminine in seeing everything "through the medium of one passion only": "There are substantial, heartfelt interests for women of all ages, and under ordinary circumstances, quite apart from love" (L, 619). Brontë reacted by breaking off the friendship, saying: "I know what *love* is as I understand it; and if man or woman should be ashamed of feeling such love, then there is nothing right, noble, faithful, truthful, unselfish in this earth" (CH, 171). Brontë was clearly sensitive to criticism. The review of *Jane Eyre* that most pleased her appeared in the influential French *Revue des deux mondes* (1848). Eugène Forçade avoided the question of authorship altogether, devoting his remarks to the political philosophy of the book, which, rather than provoking agitation as some thought, he saw as an attack on the socialist "sickness" of the time that pursues "the illusory ideal of rest under the leveller of humanitarian tyranny in order to free themselves from the proud and harsh duties of freedom and personal responsibility" (CH, 100–101). Brontë considered this "one of the most able" reviews she had ever read: "Eugène Forçade understood and enjoyed *Jane Eyre*. I cannot say that of all who professed to criticise" (CH, 100).

A month later Elizabeth Rigby summarized all the charges that had been made against the novel in England—those that called it Chartist, anti-Christian, and vulgar-minded, and altogether subversive with respect to religion, politics, and the position of women. Because Jane was "the personification of an unregenerate and undisciplined spirit" (CH, 109), her creator was assumed to be similar. In 1853, Brontë's most famous critic, Matthew Arnold, declared (after the publication of *Villette*) that her mind "contains nothing but hunger, rebellion, rage" (CH, 201). An equally famous observer, Thackeray, implied very condescendingly, that Brontë's "hunger" was sexual: "she wants some Tomkins or another to love her and be in love with. But you see she is a little bit of a creature without a penny worth of good looks, thirty years old I should think, buried in the country, and eating up her own heart there, and no Tomkins will come" (CH, 197–98). Thackeray also claimed, in typical Victorian fashion, that he could "read a great deal of her life as I fancy in her books" (CH, 197).

It was not until after Brontë's death that Elizabeth Gaskell's official biography, *The Life of Charlotte Brontë* (1857), made it necessary to revise prejudices that had persisted for ten years about the author of *Jane Eyre*. Gaskell's purpose was to exonerate her friend from the charges of "coarseness here and there in her works, otherwise so entirely noble" (L, 495), by showing that Brontë had a "strong feeling of the duty of representing life as it really is, not as it ought to be" (L, 496). Brontë's readers were assured that though she had written what George Sand called a "naughty" (L, 495) book, her own life had been morally unimpeachable. With the same vision that had informed her novels, Mrs. Gaskell presented Charlotte Brontë as a virtuous, self-sacrificing, lonely, timid woman whose commitment to writing had helped her to face constant death and sorrow. The biography, which is even today one of the most interesting that has ever been written (probably because, as Alan Shelston pointed out, Gaskell forgot "it was not a novel she was writing" [L, 29]), made a huge impact.

Brontë's critics found themselves condemned on their own grounds. "I only ask those who read [the works]," said Mrs. Gaskell, "to consider her life,—which has been openly laid bare before them" (L, 495). The author of *Jane Eyre* was then, said one incredulous reviewer, the daughter of a clergyman. George Lewes immediately wrote to Mrs. Gaskell that her book would make "a deep and permanent impression; for it . . . presents a vivid picture of a life noble and sad . . . a lesson in duty and self-reliance" (CH, 329). The *Christian Remembrancer,* which had avidly attacked Brontë, was astonished by the "startling juxtaposition" between the life and

> the preconceived conception of what the author of *Jane Eyre* must be. The genius and audacity of the story; the shrinking timidity of the writer, the decorous uneventful simplicity of the life; the bold plunge into the whirl of passion in the novel . . . how can so bashful a woman be so unbashful a writer? (CH, 364)

Canon Kingsley implied that the biography would alter critical assumptions:

> It will shame literary people into some stronger belief that a simple, virtuous, practical home life is consistent with high imaginative genius; and it will shame, too, the prudery of a not overcleanly though carefully whitewashed age, into believing that purity is now . . .

quite compatible with the knowledge of evil. I confess that the book has made me ashamed of myself.[27]

In fact, the biography effected a reversal: instead of reading, as Thackeray had done, the author's character in her novels, her work began to be read in the light of her life. It seemed that the Brontë lives were almost more fascinating than their novels. The Victorians' preference for "reality" was compounded by Mrs. Gaskell's evidence that much of *Jane Eyre* was indeed based on real experience. *The Life of Charlotte Brontë* made it very difficult to separate *Jane Eyre* from what was known of its author—a tendency that has persisted even to the present day, in spite of this century's rejection of the "biographical fallacy" of interpreting a literary work in the light of its author.

It was largely in order to supplement Gaskell's work that Clement Shorter in 1896 published biographical material he had collected as *Charlotte Brontë and Her Circle* (enlarged in 1908 to *The Brontës: Life and Letters*),[28] thus effectively pioneering Brontë studies. The 1930s saw the establishment of the Brontë canon, under the editorship of Thomas Wise and John Symington, who put together, between 1931 and 1938, the nineteen volumes of *The Shakespeare Head Brontë*,[29] including the letters, juvenilia, miscellaneous writings, and poetry of all four Brontës. Scholarship concerned itself primarily with either supplementing and questioning the biographical material (see for example the *Brontë Society Transactions*) or with interpreting the novels in the light of their increasingly known background. That Charlotte Brontë's life was considered an essential element of her fiction is attested by the many studies of the Brontës together, as though a common upbringing and background would inevitably produce similar novels.[30] One of the earliest studies of the author of *Jane Eyre* alone, E. F. Benson's *Charlotte Brontë*, has, despite its heavy biographical bias, retained a central place;[31] Mrs. Gaskell's influence seems, until recently, to have determined the emphasis of Brontë studies. From the commencement of the *Brontë Society Transactions* in 1895 to its last publication in 1972, criticism of the novels was predominantly biographical. H. E. Wroot's "Persons and Places in the Brontë

Novels," for example, published by the society in 1906, came out in book form as recently as 1970;[32] apparently some interests persist despite changes in critical theory. A glance at any Brontë bibliography will show that criticism has been largely "In the Footsteps of the Brontës" themselves (to quote the title of a work that came out in 1914).[33]

The biographical bias of Brontë criticism has frequently restricted interpretation of the novels. In 1934 Lord David Cecil declared that Brontë was "her own subject,"[34] and the idea was tenacious. Margot Peter's feminist biography *Unquiet Soul* (1975) claims that Brontë "did not know that a writer was supposed to sublimate and objectify his experience," so that her novels are filled with "her own ambivalent desires."[35] Although Helene Moglen's *Charlotte Brontë: The Self Conceived* (1976) sees the novels as mythic creations of the self and Annette Tromly's *The Cover of the Mask* (1982) further removes the novels from their author by examining the narrator's self-portraiture,[36] the idea that Brontë is a "subjective novelist"[37] has interfered with fully appreciating her artistic technique. Lord David Cecil's essay on Brontë's novels as "involuntary self-revelation," "cries of the heart," rather than "exercises of the mind,"[38] has unfortunately been highly acclaimed and frequently referred to (Margaret Blöm opens her study of Charlotte Brontë [1977] by quoting him).[39] The feminist movement of the 1960s, while offering a new perspective, somehow reinforced the Victorian identification between the author and the heroine. Margot Peter's *Unquiet Soul* even uses quotations from the novels to explain events in Brontë's life. *Jane Eyre* is seen as the outcome of Brontë's "struggle between living dutifully, and yet, as a woman of genius, unconventionally,"[40] which is essentially the same "juxtaposition" between the "timid" woman and her "audacious" genius observed over one hundred years ago by the reviewer for the *Christian Remembrancer*.

Brontë's "battle ... between conformity and rebellion"[41] is echoed in even the most recent criticism, although it has been transposed, because of the twentieth-century desire to separate a work from its author, into the text itself. Thus we find psychological, Marxist, feminist, and poststructuralist critics offering their own explanations for what they all see as a contradiction in *Jane Eyre* between its conventional surface and its subversive undercurrents.

Charles Burkhart's *Charlotte Brontë: A Psycho-sexual Study of Her Novels* (1973) answers the question of why Brontë's contemporaries thought her "vulgar and in bad taste"[42] by revealing *Jane Eyre*'s sexual symbols. Psychological criticism, by continuing to focus on the author's (albeit inner) life, can be a variant of the biographical. Robert Keefe's provocative *Charlotte Brontë's World of Death* (1979) interprets the novels in the light of "the single most important event"[43] in Brontë's life: the death of her mother. Keefe manages to avoid what John Maynard, in his excellent *Charlotte Brontë and Sexuality* (1984) calls facile "psychobiography", "in which the author's psychology is intuited out of a simplistic reading of a work, then proclaimed in itself, then reapplied to expose the real meaning of the work."[44] Brontë's work seems especially vulnerable to what Maynard calls "the perils of posthumous analysis" because so much is known of her life. Maynard proposes instead a reading of the novels themselves as "discourse on sexuality."[45]

A similarly textual analysis is undertaken from a feminist perspective by Sandra Gilbert and Susan Gubar in their impressive *The Madwoman in the Attic* (1979). They suggest that the formal language of the text is belied by a subtext betraying the "passionate drive toward freedom which offended agents of the status quo."[46] Jeannette King in her recent, excellent *Jane Eyre* gives an opposing interpretation of essentially the same textual contradiction: Jane learns, she says, that her "uncontrolled passionate feeling is unacceptable in young women" and therefore undergoes "an internalised form of repression," which creates tension between what the conclusion to the novel says and what it does: "an overt expression of certainty undercut by the narrator's self-suppression."[47] Terry Eagleton's *Myths of Power: A Marxist Study of the Brontës* (1975) sees the tensions in the text as political in origin: Brontë's aspirations to be "genteel" contradict her equally strong "contempt for all that was pampered,"[48] an ambivalence resulting from her own ambiguous social status. Mary Jacobus, employing a deconstructive approach, finds Brontë's writing linguistically subversive and contradictory because of a "doubleness" that "informs the novel as a whole."[49]

Contemporary critics seem to agree that the Victorians had cause for alarm: the formal language and ostensible moralizing suppress a disturbing subtext that undermines conventional, sexual, political and ethical values. Yet, though the "inconsistencies,"[50] as Mary Jacobus calls them, in Brontë's writing are regarded as a product of her own life's conflict, critics strangely want to divest her of responsibility for what we may call the "rebellious" aspects of her writing. The thesis that Brontë tried to conform, both artistically and morally, but couldn't, seriously undermines her artistic integrity. Robert Heilman, for example, claims that while "formally" Brontë "is for reason and real life . . . her characters keep escaping to glorify feeling and the imagination."[51] Mary Jacobus similarly claims that "the narrative and representational conventions of Victorian realism" in Brontë's writing "are constantly threatened by an incompletely repressed Romanticism."[52] Hovering behind these undeniably brilliant insights is Mrs. Gaskell's conventionally pious, even timid Brontë, attempting only to describe "real life" but somehow becoming what the Victorians called "coarse." If Brontë aspired to realism and reason, but inadvertently celebrated feeling and the imagination, she was not in control of her art, and Lord Cecil was right in calling it "involuntary self-revelation."[53] On the contrary, however, Brontë was engaged in what she called "a conscientious study of Art" when she wrote *Jane Eyre*: we will see that it was a deliberate exploration of artistic modes, as far removed from "involuntariness" as possible. *Jane Eyre*'s romanticism, its "rebellious" flight from reason, is intentional and finally predominant; but the technical experiment can only be appreciated if we forget the tradition that sees *Jane Eyre* as Brontë's autobiography and read it as the purely fictional autobiography that it is.

A
READING

– 4 –

JANE EYRE:
A "CONSCIENTIOUS STUDY OF ART"

Most criticism of *Jane Eyre* implicitly treats it as "involuntary," rather than deliberate, art. Searching Brontë's personal life for the sources of her novel is an insult to her artistic ability and a willful disregard of her aims. The title alone—*Jane Eyre: An Autobiography*—should have alerted critics to the fact that Brontë establishes, from the very beginning, the novel's independence from herself. *Jane Eyre* is a *fictional* autobiography, which is the very opposite of how it is usually regarded (i.e., as *fictionalized* autobiography). In the world created by the novel Jane is not only the narrator but the writer of the book and the "implied author" who hovers behind the work judging and informing it with her critical vision. With the device of the fictional autobiography Brontë effectively eliminates herself from the picture. Since all authorial intrusion is Jane's own, the novel is entirely self-contained and, therefore, reflects on itself. *Jane Eyre* is usually thought to describe a woman's search for personal identity, but her artistic quest is just as important as the personal. There are in fact two quests in *Jane Eyre*: that of the youthful heroine and that of the mature artist writing the autobiography. We will see that *Jane Eyre* is as much about itself and its process of being written as it is about Jane.

That Jane is the author of her own story is the single most important yet most neglected aspect of the novel. *Jane Eyre* is, like James Joyce's *A Portrait of the Artist as a Young Man,* an account of the origin and development of artistic talent, though we shall see that it has even more claim than Joyce's work to be called a "Portrait." Jane is a painter who actually illustrates for us her artistic and psychological development. Although *Jane Eyre* is customarily regarded as a fictionalized version of Brontë's personal conflicts, there is much more evidence to suggest that it dramatizes the dilemma of her artistic career.

Brontë once told W. S. Williams that the novelist has two equally important "duties": "Faithful allegiance to Truth and Nature" and such "conscientious study of Art as shall enable him to interpret eloquently and effectively" what the "oracles" reveal.[54] The "conscientious study of Art" is so important to *Jane Eyre* (and Jane Eyre) that it forms a dramatic part of the novel. Jane is a painter, unconsciously aspiring to be a writer, and we watch as her vision grows increasingly complex throughout the novel, until it is finally unable to be portrayed on canvas.

In making Jane a painter, Brontë translates into dramatic terms her own conception of the imagination. Brontë frequently felt herself to be, like the romantic visionary William Blake, a mere spectator of her fantasies: "Pen cannot portray the deep interest of the scenes . . . I have witnessed in my little room."[55] Her imagination was so strongly visual that in her youth, Elizabeth Gaskell tells us, Brontë wanted to be a painter. Like her heroine Jane, Brontë had the "right conception" to be an artist but "lacked the power of execution" in paint: "At one time, Charlotte had the notion of making her living as an artist, and wearied her eyes in drawing with pre-Raphaelite minuteness, but not with pre-Raphaelite accuracy, for she drew from fancy rather than from nature" (L, 154–55). In missing the fact that many of the Pre-Raphaelite artists frequently commenced with "fancy," Gaskell does not recognize how much Brontë's writing has in common with their art. This group of young artists who banded together in the same year that *Jane Eyre* was published used a detailed reflection of "Nature" to represent states of the soul or to reveal spiritual truths. Brontë similarly uses realistic description to convey psychological truth. This "faculty of discerning the wonderful in and through the commonplace," said one of Brontë's first reviewers, shows "the painter's eye and hand" (CH, 91–92); George Lewes reinforced this at greater lengths in terms that could apply equally well to any Pre-Raphaelite painting:

> This faculty for objective representation is also united to a strange power of subjective representation. We do not simply mean the power over the passions—the psychological intuition of the artist, but the power also of connecting external appearances with internal effects—of representing the psychological interpretation of material phenomena. (CH, 86)

The connection between "external appearances" and "internal effects," or what Brontë calls "Nature" and "Truth," is a key to her "conscientious study of Art." *Jane Eyre* analyzes the relationship between Brontë's natural romanticism (which privileges subjective imaginative perception) and her commitment to realism (or an objective presentation of external reality). In writing *Jane Eyre* Brontë resolved her artistic conflict and found her true artistic "voice."

Jane Eyre's changing ideals reflect Charlotte Brontë's artistic career. In her youth Brontë was extremely romantic: so addicted was she to her imagination that she feared it might be "a disease rather than a gift of the mind."[56] When she sent her first poems to the romantic Poet Laureate Robert Southey, he warned her that "the day-dreams in which you habitually indulge are likely to induce a distempered state of mind" (L, 172–73). Brontë tried assiduously to follow Southey's advice to "attain a degree of self-government" and "keep a quiet mind" (L, 176), especially after she had a terrifying vision of what she thought were "the ongoings of the infernal world."[57] She later told George Lewes that although she continued to write she "determined to take Nature and Truth as my sole guides, and to follow in their very footprints; I restrained imagination, eschewed romance, repressed excitement; over-bright colouring, too, I avoided" (L, 329). The result, her first novel, *The Professor,* was a failure. Advised by editors to invest her writing with more "startling incident" and "thrilling excitement" (L, 329), Brontë indulged her imagination and produced *Jane Eyre.* In writing it she seems to have resolved her previous ambivalence toward her imagination. In a letter written to George Lewes defending *Jane Eyre*'s overstepping "the real," Brontë shows unprecedented confidence in herself:

> But, dear sir, is not the real experience of each individual very limited? . . . Then, too, imagination is a strong, restless faculty, which claims to be heard and exercised: are we to be quite deaf to her cry, and insensate to her struggles? When she shows us bright pictures, are we never to look at them, and try to reproduce them? And when she is eloquent, and speaks rapidly and urgently in our ear, are we not to write to her dictation? (L, 330)

The terms in which Brontë describes her romantic conception of the irresistible authority of the imagination are extremely significant for Jane Eyre, who also sees "bright pictures" and finally, at the end of the book, opens her ears to the "cry" of her own "inspiration" (444) and acts according to it.

Jane undergoes a similar rejection, and then acceptance, of romanticism. In her childhood she is an introspective dreamer, feeding her imagination with fantastic pictures and tales, and as soon as she learns to paint she produces surrealistic dream landscapes. At Thornfield Jane clearly believes Wordsworth's principle that art (and indeed reality) "proceeds from the soul of Man, communicating its creative energies to the images of the external world."[58] She so projects her imagination onto the external world that the distinction between reality and fantasy breaks down, producing the nightmare atmosphere characteristic of Gothic horror. Jane, like Brontë, is suddenly jolted out of her fantasies by a shocking Hell-like revelation: the demonic vision of Bertha Mason (322) causes Jane's flight from the dreamworld of Thornfield to the harsh realities of the heath. At Marsh End Jane carefully avoids the dangers of romantic reverie by concentrating all

her energies on the eighteenth-century ideal of rational self-government. She produces only black-and-white realistic drawings and
avoids her previous rather "lurid" painting. In the midst of this un-
successful effort at self-control, Jane hears what she takes to be her
own inner voice calling to her (444), and she goes in search of her
former fantasy. The reunion with Rochester and the conclusion to *Jane
Eyre* are an unequivocal affirmation of the power and moral value of
Jane's imaginative intuition. At the end of her own writing career
Brontë explained, using the images that permeate *Jane Eyre,* that her
imagination had been her own salvation:

> The faculty of imagination lifted me when I was sinking. . . . its
> active exercise has kept my head above water since. . . . I am thank-
> ful to God, who gave me the faculty; and it is for me a part of my
> religion to defend this gift, and to profit by its possession.
> (L, 383)

Whenever Brontë describes her creative powers she employs
either geographical metaphors ("follow in their footsteps," "keep
my head above water") or the terminology of visual art ("scenes,"
"bright pictures"). These near-clichés are Brontë's colloquial terms
for the more sophisticated conception of the artistic process, which
is worked out in *Jane Eyre.* The two metaphors around which *Jane
Eyre* is constructed are that of the journey and that of self-portrait:
Jane's journey in search of her personal and artistic identity is the constant central motif that is interspersed with momentary self-revelations in the form of "self-portraits." Jane's mental development in the
autobiography is gradually revealed through the changing landscape
that reflects her vision of the world. This linear movement of the text
is augmented by sudden insights into Jane's inner life that create a
multifaceted "portrait" of her hidden self. The mature Jane recognizes
in retrospect the extent to which she once fashioned the world
according to her subjective desires. The autobiographer sees what
Jane does not—that the places she inhabits and the people she knows
reflect and sometimes embody her inner life, so that character and

setting have a metaphoric as well as a purely naturalistic function in the text.

The extensive description of landscape, houses, gardens and even the weather in *Jane Eyre* consistently indicates Jane's mental state. It is difficult to say whether Jane's physical condition mirrors the mental one or vice versa, because the landscape described in *Jane Eyre* switches, sometimes imperceptibly, from outer to inner and is usually both at once, as for example when Jane wishes to travel beyond the "blue peaks" she can see from Lowood (117), or when Rochester threatens to carry her to "the edge of a crater" (295). Like Christian in *Pilgrim's Progress* Jane travels through her own "Valley of the Shadow of Death" and "Delectable Mountains" representing states of the soul. Gateshead, Lowood, Thornfield, Whitcross, Marsh End, and Ferndean symbolize, as their names suggest, the "genius" of place, and they represent Jane's condition while she inhabits them. The characters also, whom Rochester says appear like "shapes" in the "magic lantern" (227) of Jane's own vision, are frequently projections of her hopes and fears. Jane constantly confronts otherwise unrecognized aspects of herself in mirrors, her own painting, or characters who function momentarily as doubles. The consistent analogy in *Jane Eyre* between the house, garden, and wider landscape with regions of the mind establishes a parallel between the young Jane's exploration of the world and the mature writer's exploration of her self.

Landscape and self-portrait converge in the characteristic and important landscape paintings that Jane executes at Lowood and describes in detail when she arrives at Thornfield. Each isolated figure emerging from the natural elements of fire, water, ice, and rock represents not only Jane's inner life but also Brontë's own conception of the creative faculty that she once described as a sculptor "hewing" statues, or fictional characters, out of the elements of the mind (CH, 287). This statement, describing the nature of her sister Emily's inspiration, forms part of Brontë's most illuminating comments on the novelist's art (CH, 284–88).

In defending Emily Brontë on the one hand, and attacking Jane Austen on the other, Brontë situates her own art using the same images that inform *Jane Eyre*. Austen's *Pride and Prejudice*, she says, is like "an accurate daguerreotyped portrait of a commonplace face; a carefully fenced, highly cultivated garden, with neat borders and delicate flowers; but no glance of a bright, vivid physiognomy, no open country."[59] Brontë here combines the metaphors of portrait and place in order to define Austen's art. Because it is a photographic likeness, it misses, says Brontë, "what throbs fast and full, though hidden, what the blood rushes through, what is the unseen seat of life and the sentient target of death—this Miss Austen ignores."[60] Brontë blames the limitations of Jane Austen's vision on her unwillingness to leave the "carefully-fenced, highly-cultivated garden" of common sense.

If Jane Austen has no "open country," Emily Brontë perhaps has too much. Brontë defends the uncouth Heathcliff in *Wuthering Heights* as springing inevitably from the rude country that fed Emily's imagination. Because her sister was "a native and nursling of the moors," explained Charlotte, her art was inevitably "moorish, and wild, and knotty as a root of heath" (CH, 285). In *Jane Eyre* Brontë takes her heroine out of the garden and onto the heath, and thus effects an exploration of the remote regions of mind, beyond the limitations of naturalistic art. Brontë once declared that George Lewes was unable to go

> beyond a certain intellectual limit; the mystery will never be cleared up to you, for that limit you will never overpass. Not all your learning, not all your reading, not all your sagacity, not all your perseverance can help you over one viewless line—one boundary as impassable as it is invisible. To enter that sphere a man must be born within it.[61]

With the device of fictional autobiography, Brontë achieves a "conscientious study of Art" in *Jane Eyre*. Because Jane is the author, as well as the narrator and heroine of her own story, she tells it self-consciously. Throughout the novel the reader is constantly invited to reflect on the process of telling the story, not least by the famous direct addresses to the "Reader." These perform the dual function of simultaneously creating and destroying the fictional illusion: although they inspire a sense of intimacy with the heroine (rather like whispering gossip into the reader's ear) they also remind us that we *are* readers and that this is a work of art: "Stay till he comes, reader; and, when I disclose my secret to him, you shall share the confidence" (304). More important, Jane explores, within the novel, different ways of presenting the subject matter of her life: not only the paintings and drawings, which are visual representations of Jane's often limited perspective on events, but also many other devices throughout the novel imitate, and therefore reveal, the limitations of the storytelling. A summary of the devices of "repetition" in *Jane Eyre* illustrates the extent to which the novel is a "conscientious study of Art":

1. The paintings and drawings, which indicate the changing style and artistic ideals of each section, and reveal Jane's inner life.

2. Other visual images of Jane's self in mirrors, or in characters who function as doubles (Rochester as the gypsy, Adèle), or fancied reflection in mirrors (Bertha Mason on the eve of Jane's wedding); all of which offer a multifaceted "portrait" of Jane's inner self.

3. Dreams, which combine the landscape analogy of the paintings with characters who represent doppelgängers (e.g., Jane dreams of clutching a baby in a crumbling house).

4. The charades, a species of "play within the play" that prove to be prophetic ("Bridewell").

5. Passages in which others are writing or relating their own autobiographies in such a way that they throw light on Jane's (Rochester, who actually writes his history and spends many hours relating parts of it to Jane, and who turns it into a fairy-story for Adèle; St John, who tells Jane that his own spiritual history has been like hers).

6. Passages in which Jane's story is related to her by others (Rochester and St John both describe their early voyeuristic observations of Jane's ways); and specifically when St John tells Jane "Elliott" all about Jane Eyre.

7. Bessie's and Rochester's ballads, which are quoted in full, and which are remarkably similar to Jane's situation.

8. The picture books in which Jane intuitively senses characteristics akin to her own.

9. The parody of the wedding ceremony, which Jane reverses and negates in order to extricate herself from Rochester.
10. Jane's own "thrice told tale" of the red-room incident, in which each telling is different.

All these parodic devices balance "Nature" (or the realistic illusion of life) with "Truth" (or the underlying spiritual, emotional drama): "Oh romantic reader, forgive me for telling the plain truth!" (141), says Jane of one of the most symbolic characters, Grace Poole. Brontë thus employs a naturalistic illusion of real life for symbolic purposes; but we will see that the romantic aspect of the novel finally predominates over the realistic. Perhaps the strongest evidence of *Jane Eyre*'s romanticism is that it avoids theorizing about art while reflecting on it. Unlike James Joyce's novel, Brontë's truly does present a "*portrait* of the artist" that indicates, without explicitly discussing, the protagonist's youthful development. It is largely through the devices of visual parody that the "study of Art" is implicitly achieved. Thus, when Brontë was asked by her editors for explanations of certain parts of *Jane Eyre* she reprimanded them in terms that exactly characterize her artistic vision:

> I might explain away a few other points, but it would be too much like drawing a picture and then writing underneath the name of the object intended to be represented. We know what sort of a pencil that is which needs an ally in the pen. (L, 485–86)

– 5 –

GATESHEAD:
OUT OF THE GARDEN

Jane's search for a personal and artistic identity takes her from Gateshead to Lowood, Thornfield, Whitcross, Marsh End, and finally Ferndean, each habitation corresponding to a stage in her mental development and therefore in her artistic vision. In order to pursue Jane through this changing landscape of her life it seems advisable to adopt a linear reading of the narrative combined with vertical plunges into its underlying symbolism. In this way we can bring to light what Jane does not recognize at the time the events take place—their significance for her artistic and psychic development.

Near the beginning of the book Jane warns that her life story will be highly selective according to her mature interests:

> This is not to be a regular autobiography: I am only bound to invoke memory where I know her responses will possess some degree of interest; therefore I now pass a space of eight years almost in silence: a few lines only are necessary to keep up the links of connexion. (115)

The reader is reminded that the "I" is an author, making deliberate decisions about "chapters": "Hitherto I have recorded in detail the events of my insignificant existence: to the first ten years of my life I have given almost as many chapters" (115). It is clear from the events she chooses to relate that the "degree of interest" they have for the autobiographer is their influence on her later development. The mature Jane records her childhood in detail because she is searching for the origins of her artistic talent.

Gateshead is appropriately named for Jane's beginning since it combines the idea of a threshold, a passing out through the "gates," with that of birth (head first). From the very opening paragraph, Jane is wandering in a bleak landscape representative of her psychological condition: "We had been wandering . . . in the leafless shrubbery an hour" (39). Jane is fundamentally a nomad—an orphan with no roots and little knowledge of her beginnings. It is this that inspires her archetypically Victorian search for identity: Jane is ejected (like her mythical grandparents) beyond the "gates" into the wide unknown. At Gateshead Jane is dragged out from her hiding place behind the curtains, is locked in the red-room (epitomizing her mental imprisonment), and then released, first into the garden (which symbolizes her transition from interiority), then onto a road of "preter-natural length" (74) for a journey that, like birth, commences in darkness (73).

In the memory of the autobiographer the time at Gateshead is perpetual winter. The connection between Jane's inner and outer landscapes is established in the very opening of the novel: she is as vulnerable to the "penetrating" rain (39) as to the hostility of those around her. The "raw twilight" (39) seems to persist for the whole novel, relieved by very few flashes of sunlight. Jane lacks emotional as well as physical warmth, excluded from the family circle clustered around the "fireside" (39). When she hides behind the window curtains, Jane is "shrined" in the "double retirement" (39) of her physical sanctuary and her own mind (which she travels over in solitude). From here she looks through "the clear panes of glass, protecting, but not separating me from the drear November day" (39). Though she turns from people to nature, Jane is so timid that she cannot realize her need to escape, and she can only gaze at the world through the window. Furthermore, her vulnerability and habitual mood of depression make the whole world seem cold and inhospitable. Jane's alienation increases as Mrs.

Reed's "eye of ice continued to dwell freezingly on mine" (68), so that even the glass panes become frozen-over, making it impossible to see beyond her immediate petrified self: "I fell to breathing on the frost-flowers with which the window was fretted, and thus clearing a space in the glass through which I might look out on the grounds, where all was still and petrified under the influence of a hard frost" (62). As the mature Jane begins her autobiography she is paralyzed by the recollection of her early fears and can only glimpse the garden that she will later explore.

THE ORIGIN OF HER ARTISTIC TALENT

Jane's early alienation has far-reaching consequences for her later talents. At the beginning of her life she is, like Robert Browning's artist-hero Fra Lippo Lippi, forced by deprivation to become acutely perceptive:

> When a boy starves in the streets
> Eight years together as my fortune was,
> Watching folks' faces to know who will fling
> The bit of half-sipped grape bunch he desires,
> And who will kick or curse him for his pains,—
>
> Why, soul and sense of him grow sharp alike.
> He learns the look of things, and none the less
> For admonition from the hunger-pinch.
> I had a store of such remarks, be sure,
> Which, after I found leisure, turned to use.[62]

Fra Lippo Lippi consequently became an artist who could convey "soul" through "sense." Jane must similarly be constantly on her guard to avoid being "kicked or cursed" by her cousins, so that she too learns to assess human nature by observing external appearance, a faculty that is employed throughout her book. Jane remains detached even while being mistreated by her cousin John: "I knew he would soon strike, and while dreading the blow, I mused on the disgusting and ugly appearance of him who would presently deal it" (42). Jane cannot help being amused by the grotesque gargoyle face in front of her. Even on the first page she is able to satirize the family in a manner that anticipates her later debunking of the guests at Thornfield:

> The said Eliza, John, and Georgiana were now clustered round their mamma in the drawing-room: she lay reclined on a sofa by the fireside, and with her darlings about her (for the time neither quarrelling nor crying) looked perfectly happy. Me, she had dispensed from joining the group. (39)

Thus Jane's silent observation of all that goes on around her is not without its sense of humor.

In her loneliness Jane turns to books, and so begins the love of literature and art that carries her through an otherwise unhappy early life. Significantly it is Bessie the maid, the only person to show Jane affection at Gateshead, who initiates Jane's childhood love of stories. Jane's only memory of comfort is when Bessie, ironing by the fire, "fed our eager attention with passages of love and adventure taken from old fairy tales and older ballads; or (as at a later period I discovered) from the pages of *Pamela,* and *Henry, Earl of Moreland*" (41). These memories influence Jane for the rest of her life; the three girls who become her most intimate friends are all reading when she first sets eyes on them. Her desire to know Helen Burns at Lowood is aroused because she sees her reading Johnson's *Rasselas* (82), and in the first vision of Diana and Mary in domestic bliss at Marsh End they are reading German poetry aloud (358–59). It is not surprising that at Gateshead Jane's books are as important to her as the doll "shabby as a miniature scarecrow" (61) on which she showers affection. What she doesn't recognize is that the little "faded graven image" (61) is an image of herself, and similarly the books, stories, and ballads of her childhood offer figures with whom she unconsciously identifies. One of Bessie's ballads is recalled in full by the autobiographer and thus serves as an early self-parody. The sentimental and sensationalized rendering of the plight of "the poor orphan child" suggests Jane's tendency to melodramatize her situation, but it is also prophetic of her later journey:

> Why did they send me so far and so lonely,
> Up where the moors spread and gray rocks
> are piled? (54)

Gulliver, "a most desolate wanderer in most dread and dangerous regions" (53), is similarly a fictional favorite of Jane's who reflects her own condition.

Almost as soon as *Jane Eyre* opens we find Jane lost in the "solitary rocks and promontories" of Bewick's *History of British Birds* (40), but she is unable to explain the fascination of "those forlorn regions of dreary space": "Of these death-white realms I formed an idea of my own: shadowy, like all the half-comprehended notions that float dim through children's brains, but strangely impressive." (40). It is no mere coincidence that, when Jane learns to paint, she repeats these symbols of her inner fears: the "broken boat stranded on a desolate coast," the "rock standing up alone in a sea of billow," the "fields of ice," "Alpine heights," and even the "black, horned thing" (40), all recur in the paintings described in detail to the reader in chapter 13 (157). At this stage of her life, however, Jane is so paralyzed by self-doubt that she has no creative initiative and can only feed her imagination with images others have created.

Jane's early love of literature encourages her, on the one hand, to make comparisons with her situation, but on the other hand, to embroider that situation with her strong imagination. What she calls her ability to draw "parallels" (43) between literature and her own life is combined with an equally strong inability to distinguish between the two—a tendency that persists throughout her recorded life and becomes especially dangerous at Thornfield. Jane's reading enables her to recognize her oppression: her bullying cousin John is the tyrannical figure described in Goldsmith's *History of Rome* (43), but this makes Jane into the "revolted slave" (46). Because she says so, Jane is locked, as punishment, in the red-room, and her life really does begin to resemble literature as she enters a region "chill . . . silent . . . remote . . . solemn, because it was known to be so seldom entered" (45).

THE SELF-PORTRAIT IN THE RED-ROOM

In the red-room Jane sees herself as a rebellious slave, a hunger-striker, the "scapegoat of the nursery" (47), and the orphan child locked up by the wicked stepmother. "No doubt," says the autobiographer in retrospect, "I was a precocious actress" in the eyes of her aunt (49), thereby drawing attention to her self-dramatization. Throughout her childhood Jane has been inexplicably attracted by disguised portraits of herself in books, ballads, and her doll; in the red-room she is confronted with an obvious self-portrait in the mirror, giving her a new awareness of her own identity. We are prepared for the significance of the mirror by the fact that when John "throws the book" at Jane, metaphorically as well as literally, he symbolically deprives her of any sense of herself not only by emphasizing her absence of rights, but by making her move "out of the way of the mirror and the windows" (42). Throughout the novel, mirrors and windows offer Jane glimpses into her inner world. In the red-room it is clearly her subliminal self that appears in the old looking glass:

> I had to cross before the looking-glass; my fascinated glance involuntarily explored the depth it revealed. All looked colder and darker in that visionary hollow than in reality: and the strange little figure there gazing at me with a white face and arms specking the gloom, and glittering eyes of fear moving where all else was still, had the effect of a real spirit: I thought it like one of the tiny phantoms, half fairy, half imp, Bessie's evening stories represented as coming out of lone, ferny dells in moors, and appearing before the eyes of belated travellers. (46)

The "visionary hollow" is as much a reflection of Jane's interior as it is of the room. This first explicit self-portrait combines the metaphor of landscape with that of the portrait that we find in the later paintings and throughout the novel, but at this stage Jane is no more substantial than "air" or "Eyre" and could not be portrayed on canvas. Jane so little knows or understands her internal aspect that she does not recognize herself. The first identification of oneself in a mirror is regarded by Jacques Lacan[63] as the most decisive stage in human development, constituting the awareness of oneself as an object of knowledge. Although the reflection is a misrepresentation, because static, it nevertheless confers the mark of adulthood: self-consciousness. But Jane's perception of herself is colored by what she calls "superstition": all the previous injustice "turned up in my disturbed mind like a dark deposit in a turbid well" (46). Recalling her uncle Reed who had abandoned her to this fate, Jane becomes so terrified that "a ghost would come" (49) that she loses consciousness, but it is her own imagination, nothing more, that causes her fear.

THE UNCANNY IN *JANE EYRE*

Jane knew that her fear was caused by a "disturbed mind" turning up its dark deposits: the image is a remarkable anticipation of Freud's belief that the unconscious is the repository of repressed emotions that nevertheless resurface in distorted forms. Until the crisis in the red-room Jane has not admitted to hating the family to whom she should be grateful. Her combined horror and fascination for the "black horned thing" in her picture book "surveying a distant crowd surrounding a gallows" (40) is, however, clearly a projection of her unacknowledged desire for revenge. The image of herself in the mirror is similarly distorted. Such doubles, says Freud, are external manifestations of repressed desires: "all the strivings of the ego which adverse external circumstances have crushed." Because the moralistic ego censors hostile feelings, they become projected onto an apparently external object; it is "the urge towards defence which has caused the ego to project that material outward as something foreign to itself."[64] Throughout her life Jane is crushed by external circumstances, but the frustration and resentment that arise from these experiences cannot find an outlet, because her dependency deprives her of any sense of entitlement. When Jane attacks and accuses her aunt Reed she later feels guilty because her conscience, which is socialized and therefore judges herself as others would, cannot condone such behavior. The initial effect of admitting to hating her aunt is one of relief, followed by intensified guilt:

> A child cannot quarrel with its elders, as I had done—cannot give its furious feelings uncontrolled play, as I had given mine—without experiencing afterwards the pang of remorse and the chill of reaction. . . .
>
> Something of vengeance I had tasted for the first time. An aromatic wine it seemed, on swallowing, warm and racy; its after-flavour, metallic and corroding, gave me a sensation as if I had been poisoned. (69–70)

The taste of victory is poisoned by guilt, so Jane once more crushes her violent emotions. When she "lets go" and accuses her aunt it is as though another self speaks: "it seemed as if my tongue pronounced words without my will consenting to their utterance: something spoke out of me over which I had no control" (60). This other self is "savage": " 'Deceit is not my fault!' I cried out in a savage, high voice" (69). Throughout the book, Jane projects emotions of intense resentment that she cannot condone in herself and does not like to admit. At Thornfield the same psychological pattern is repeated in an intensified form. Both Bertha Mason, "the foul German spectre—the vampire" (311) that Jane sees in the mirror at Thornfield, and the phantom, "half fairy, half imp" (46) that she now sees in the mirror at Gateshead, are what Freud called "Uncanny" figures: manifestations of that which should have remained hidden but is shockingly revealed.[65]

The crisis in the red-room, then, is Jane's first lesson in self-awareness, and it causes her "fall" from childhood innocence into recognition of her own potential evil. The autobiographer, reminding us of her authorial presence, explicitly searches for metaphors of her childish anger: "A ridge of lighted heath, alive, glancing, devouring, would have been a great emblem of my mind when I accused and menaced Mrs. Reed" (69). What at this stage are mere "emblems" of Jane's inner life become increasingly autonomous and take on a dramatic reality as the writer becomes more daring in her self-exploration.

THE STORYTELLER'S FIRST LESSON

This explicit search for metaphors of her inner life is only one of the many ways in which the autobiographer draws attention to her own storytelling. Just before the account of the red-room crisis the mature Jane intercepts the narrative (with an explicitly anachronistic intrusion) to tell us that she sees things very differently in retrospect:

> Now, at the distance of—I will not say how many years—I see it clearly.
>
> I was a discord at Gateshead Hall; I was like nobody there. . . . They were not bound to regard with affection a thing that could not sympathize with one amongst them. (47)

She thus implicitly warns us of the young Jane's bias. The events of the red-room are recounted four times by Jane, and each telling is modified by her current attitudes. When we witness Jane blurting out to her aunt, the apothecary, Helen Burns, and Miss Temple, we already know the event (the first account in the book is the last in the fictional time of the autobiographer). By her third telling Jane has learned a lesson that she carries with her into her later career as a writer: that a "plain tale with few pretensions" (35), as "Currer Bell" describes it in the preface, is more believable than a fervent one.

Jane's first representation of the incident, intended to condemn her aunt, is by far the most impassioned:

I shall remember how you thrust me back—roughly and violently thrust me back—into the red-room, and locked me up there, to my dying day, though I was in agony, though I cried out, while suffocating with distress, "Have mercy! Have mercy Aunt Reed!" . . . I will tell anybody who asks me questions this exact tale. (68–69)

The words "and locked me up there, to my dying day" create an appropriate ambiguity: for Jane the loss of consciousness *was* a kind of death. The exaggeration is perhaps justified, but Jane does not always tell this "exact tale." When questioned by the "good apothecary" she tells him that what her aunt did was "so cruel that I think I shall never forget it" (55): "I was shut up in a room where there is a ghost, till after dark" (55). His reaction reflects the ambivalence of the mature Jane (especially as she has such fond memories of his judiciousness) and shows her capable of self-irony: "I saw Mr. Lloyd smile and frown at the same time: 'Ghost! What, you are a baby after all! You are afraid of ghosts?' " (55).

The next, even less sympathetic listener, is Helen Burns. Jane proceeds "forthwith to pour out, in my own way, the tale of my sufferings and resentments. Bitter and truculent when excited, I spoke as I felt, without reserve or softening" (90). Having heard Jane "patiently to the end," Helen observes "how minutely" she remembers all her aunt's injustice: "Would you not be happier if you tried to forget her severity, together with the passionate emotions it excited? Life appears to me too short to be spent in nursing animosity or registering wrongs" (90). From Helen Jane learns the first lesson of her artistic career. By the time she unburdens herself to Miss Temple, the story is significantly different:

I resolved in the depth of my heart, that I would be most moderate—most correct; and, having reflected a few minutes in order to arrange coherently what I had to say, I told her all the story of my sad childhood. Exhausted by emotion, my language was more subdued than it generally was when it developed that sad theme; and mindful of Helen's warnings against the indulgence of resentment, I infused into the narrative far less of gall and wormwood than ordinary. Thus restrained and simplified, it sounded more credible: I felt as I went on that Miss Temple fully believed me. (102–3)

Miss Temple's reaction, her immediate declaration that Jane is cleared from guilt, so impresses Jane that it influences even her writing. Although "nothing could soften in my recollection the spasm of agony" she had felt at being pushed back into "the dark and haunted chamber" (103), she nevertheless resolves that from then on she would tell the "story of my sad childhood" in as "subdued" language as possible.

THE JOURNEY COMMENCES

The next thing Jane remembers after the terrifying red-room experience is "waking up with a feeling as if I had had a frightful nightmare" (51); but what she wakens to is a new sense of self, remarked by Bessie: "You sharp little thing! You've got quite a new way of talking. What makes you so venturesome and hardy?" (71). The difference is that an "invisible bond" had broken, freeing Jane from her cowering submission. When she defends herself from her aunt, her "soul began to expand, to exult, with the strangest sense of freedom, of triumph, I ever felt. It seemed as if an invisible bond had burst, and that I had struggled out into unhoped-for liberty" (69). Freed from her previous fears, Jane passes through the unseen barrier that had prevented her exploration of the world and herself:

> I opened the glass-door in the breakfast-room: the shrubbery was quite still: the black frost reigned, unbroken by sun or breeze, through the grounds. I covered my head and arms with the skirt of my frock, and went out to walk . . . ; but I found no pleasure in the silent trees, the falling fir-cones, the congealed relics of autumn, russet leaves swept by past winds in heaps, and now stiffened together. (70)

Although Jane is still protecting herself with a kind of curtain (her lifted skirt) she has nevertheless taken the first step in search of herself.

Gateshead

In the garden of Gateshead Jane undergoes a physical and spiritual transition away from the "visionary hollow" of her inner confinement. The pattern is repeated at Thornfield, after Jane has explored beyond the gates and is unwilling to return to the "gloomy house," the "gray hollow" (148), which she can see through the glass doors. In each incident the windows function as the "invisible boundary" dividing the imprisoned mind from its imaginative liberty. Jane's longing to transcend her physical constraints is typically romantic (see Keats's "Ode to a Nightingale," for example); she aspires to flight, but cannot escape: "little things recall us to earth: the clock struck in the hall" (148).

Although Jane's landscape is unpromisingly bleak—a "black frost reigned" (70)—it will become less barren as she becomes more mentally fertile. Jane is about to be ejected from the garden of Gateshead and childhood: her aunt has arranged for her to go to Lowood school. Thus commences the journey that will take her to increasingly remote regions of nature and her own mind.

– 6 –

LOWOOD:
THE WIDENING VISION

Lowood, the first stage of Jane's journey out into the world, is also the place of the greatest transition in Jane's life, from childhood to adolescence (she is at the school from the ages of ten to eighteen). At Lowood Jane confronts the harsh reality of physical survival, which focuses some of her previous introspective thoughts. Although events at Lowood are correspondingly described in the "plain" terms that Jane has learned are so effective, the result is, like T. S. Eliot's *The Waste Land,* a panorama of a hellish existence. Despite terrible deprivation, however, Jane is given something at Lowood far more precious than the food and clothing she had at Gateshead: a sense of her own worth.

Released from her paralyzing childhood fears, Jane's sense of self becomes more substantial, thus prompting the most significant change of her life. Jane learns to paint, and this is the commencement of her future career. Lowood is appropriately named as the starting point of Jane's ascent, since it is both literally and metaphorically "a cradle of fog and fog-bred pestilence" (108), where occurs one of the lowest, indeed suicidal, events in Jane's life: "could I ever rise more?" (100). Jane does, however, "stand" once more after her identity crisis, which is both more intense and more decisive than the one at Gateshead. From that point on she becomes more confident and optimistic. The new "prospect" in Jane's life is represented by the weather, which, despite an eight-year stay at the school, changes only once from perpetual winter to bright spring.

Jane's journey to the school begins in cold and darkness before dawn in the first month of the year, clearly signifying a kind of birth— "I remember but little of the journey; I only know that the day seemed to me of preternatural length" (74)—suggesting admittance to a new future: "Gathering my faculties, I looked about me. Rain, wind, and darkness filled the air, nevertheless, I dimly discerned a wall before me and a door open in it" (75).

The first months at Lowood, in the autobiographer's memory, are as desolate as her time at Gateshead: "My first quarter at Lowood seemed an age, and not the golden age either; . . . the deep snows . . . the almost impassable roads, prevented our stirring beyond the garden walls" (92). Jane is still confined to the garden walls and to an impoverished vision. Frozen by fear, she remains vulnerable to the hostile universe: "we returned by an exposed and hilly road, where the bitter wind . . . almost flayed the skin from our faces" (92). She tries to protect herself, as she had at Gateshead, in "double retirement":

> my gray mantle close about me, and, trying to forget the cold which nipped me without, and the unsatisfied hunger which gnawed me within, delivered myself up to the employment of watching and thinking. My reflections were too undefined and fragmentary to merit record. I hardly yet knew where I was. Gateshead and my past life seemed floated away to an immeasurable distance. The present was vague and strange, and of the future I could form no conjecture. (81)

Jane's spiritual and physical hunger, however, is relieved when the sense of oppression she carries with her from Gateshead is lifted; when she is pronounced guiltless by the headmistress of Lowood, her metaphorical wounds heal with her physical ones: "My wretched feet, flayed and swollen to lameness by the sharp air of January, began to heal and subside under the gentler breathings of April" (107). Jane's view of the garden is explicitly linked to her mental "outlook": the lawns, "freshening daily, suggested the thought that Hope traversed them at night, and left each morning brighter traces of her steps" (107). Jane becomes mentally as well as physically more adventurous:

> I discovered too, that a great pleasure, an enjoyment which the horizon only bounded, lay all outside the high and spike-guarded walls of our garden: this pleasure consisted in prospect of noble summits girdling a great hill-hollow, rich in verdure and shadow. (107)

Jane discovers that she can escape even the iron rule of Lowood into her own unlimited freedom. By the end of her stay at Lowood, Jane is no longer content with the scope of the horizon—a pattern that repeats itself throughout the autobiography, each time propelling her beyond the limits of her vision.

The effect of Jane's psychological state on her view of things is explicitly recalled by the autobiographer: "How different had this scene looked when I viewed it laid out beneath the iron sky of winter, stiffened in frost, shrouded with snow!" (107). The change occurs in Jane only after her recognition of a lack of self-reliance, of firm ground within herself.

THE SEARCH FOR A GROUND

Because Jane lacks a distinct sense of herself, she is, as Helen Burns points out, extremely dependent on the approval of others. This tendency persists, in lessening degrees, throughout her life; it is only after a long struggle with stronger personalities that Jane's own identity fully emerges. In childhood, the major influence on her moral or psychological growth is religion; the spectrum of Christian beliefs is presented to her in the form of various figures for possible emulation. From Brocklehurst's self-righteous hypocrisy to Helen Burns's self-effacing martyrdom, to Miss Temple's unostentatious self-denial, Jane seeks a place for herself, a ground for her own faith, but finds none. She finally rejects all the proffered religious positions for her own (un-articulated) convictions. Even as a child, Jane has idiosyncratic tastes that are construed as heretical: when Brocklehurst asks whether she likes the Psalms, she replies that they are "not interesting" (65), which "proves," says Brocklehurst, that she has "a wicked heart" (65). Early reviewers considered Jane anti-Christian: it is true that the novel attacks conventional religion and describes Jane's search for her own beliefs, and in doing so it challenges Victorian religious practices. The Reverend Brocklehurst's advocacy of Christian doctrine is unattended by any Christian "agape" or love of fellows. He uses religion, on the contrary, to justify cruelty: he is the paradigm Pharisee condemned in the preface (35).

Helen Burns, at the other end of the religious spectrum, is a martyr, a victim of the clergy-school's practice of chastising the flesh for the sake of the soul. Helen Burns is nevertheless the ideal to which all Victorian girls were exhorted: submissive, obedient, and acquiescent in the sufferings of this life because she has her sights fixed on the next: "I live in calm, looking to the end" (91). The novel "exposes" Helen as much as it does Brocklehurst; and although Jane respects Helen and Miss Temple alike, she finds herself unable to follow their example. By the end of her stay at Lowood School, Jane discovers that she does not endorse the Christian principle of self-sacrifice. She rejects all the religious examples that have been offered to her, in the unarticulated conviction that oppressing the body oppresses the soul. Perhaps Brontë shocked her contemporaries because her "realistic symbolism" celebrates the body as well as the soul (like Browning's Fra Lippo Lippi).

It is Brocklehurst, the intimidating president of Lowood School, who argues most strongly that "If ye suffer hunger and thirst for My sake, happy are ye" (95), but it is a purely theoretical position, exposed by his obviously affluent and self-indulgent family. His armchair Christianity is no more than a convenient justification for depriving the Lowood pupils: "Oh, madam, when you put bread and cheese, instead of burnt porridge, into these children's mouths, you may indeed feed their vile bodies, but you little think how you starve their immortal souls!" (95).

The result is that Lowood is a living hell for its inhabitants. When Jane first surveys the scene in the refectory it seems to her like Milton's description of the hissing fallen angels in *Paradise Lost*: "I saw a universal manifestation of discontent when the fumes of the repast met the nostrils of those destined to swallow it" (77–78). By way of contrast, when Jane is offered seed-cake in Miss Temple's study, she feels she is in Heaven: "We feasted that evening as on nectar and ambrosia" (104). Lowood institution, in the name of salvation, deprives its pupils even of their female identity by cutting off their curls and dressing them uniformly in brown. Bullied into conformity, the girls seem to have a corporate identity: "the whole school rose simultaneously, as if moved by a common spring" (79). Helen Burns, whom Jane befriends, is a model Lowood pupil at the cost, finally, of her life. She counters Brocklehurst's and Miss Scatcherd's brutality by turning the other cheek: "I could not comprehend this doctrine of endurance," says Jane, "still less could I understand or sympathize with the forbearance she expressed for her chastiser" (88). Jane's strong sense of injustice, carried with her from her Gateshead experiences, will not allow her to be another Helen Burns, whose death is an implicit indictment of what amounts to martyrdom.

Jane is more tempted to emulate the principal of Lowood School, Miss Temple, who quietly practices Christian dedication to others. She resists Brocklehurst with masklike, statuesque composure:

> but she now gazed straight before her, and her face, naturally pale as marble, appeared to be assuming also the coldness and fixity of that material; especially her mouth, closed as if it would have required a sculptor's chisel to open it, and her brow settled gradually into petrified severity. (95)

The sculptural metaphor is interesting; Brocklehurst has already been compared by Jane to "a black pillar" (63), and here Miss Temple is established as a pure white antidote to the minister's "black" soul. But her resistance is achieved by an emotional petrifaction that Jane could not tolerate. (In the next section we see that Jane herself also becomes a rival statue.)

When Helen Burns dies, and Jane's support is removed, she tries to find a solid ground of faith within herself, but she experiences only a vertiginous terror:

> My mind made its first earnest effort to comprehend what had been infused into it concerning heaven and hell . . . it saw all round an unfathomed gulf: it felt the one point where it stood—the present; all the rest was formless cloud and vacant depth; and it shuddered at the thought of tottering, and plunging amid that chaos. (110–11)

By the time Miss Temple marries and her influence is removed, Jane is able to acknowledge that her own aspirations are different from her teacher's:

> With her was gone every settled feeling. . . . I had imbibed from her something of her nature and much of her habits; more harmonious thoughts. . . . I had given in allegiance to duty and order; I was quiet . . . I appeared a disciplined and subdued character. (116)

The strongest influences of Jane's childhood, then, are the various Christian principles practiced at Lowood School. Helen Burns and Miss Temple offer tempting examples for Jane, but their resignation is not for her: she knows that she only outwardly assents to the role prescribed for Victorian women by conventional religion. Jane has, throughout her stay at Lowood, paid lip service to "duty and order," but the "reason for tranquility" (116) is removed with Miss Temple, allowing a returning flood of Jane's more authentic emotions: "I remembered that the real world was wide, and that a varied field of hopes and fears, of sensations and excitements, awaited those who had courage to go forth into its expanse, to seek real knowledge of life amidst its perils" (116). At Lowood Jane rejects the ultimately fatal constraints of the institution and of Christian self-denial in favor of the romantic principles of sensation and experience. It is not until the end of the novel, when Jane aggressively attacks St John, that she articulates her belief that denying the body kills the soul, but the ideal is present throughout the novel in its attempt to formulate a kind of spiritual naturalism (which is why the Victorians thought it "animalistic"). It takes Jane a long time to reject authority in favor of her own judgment, but her punishment by Brocklehurst at Lowood School enables her to recognize that she need not be defined by others.

THE "LIAR" ON THE STOOL

Jane's punishment by Brocklehurst is the second major visual presentation of herself in the novel, but unlike the looking-glass portrait, it is formulated and fashioned by someone else and is even further removed from the truth. As a result of it, however, Jane learns to reject the "picture" of herself that others attempt to impose on her (a lesson that later enables her to preserve her identity in the face of Rochester's and St John's illusions). Brocklehurst attempts to make Jane into the "Liar," a living illustration to the *Child's Guide* he had given her at Gateshead. In words that recall Brontë's conception of the artist "sculpting" characters out of the imagination, Jane describes herself as a statue on a "pedestal of infamy" (99) to rival the "black pillar" (63) of Brocklehurst. First Jane had thought Brocklehurst a piece of grotesque architecture—"the grim face at the top was like a carved mask, placed above the shaft by way of capital" (63)—but she is now, significantly, raised to the level of the "black marble clergyman's" nose (98). The autobiographer, distanced from the immediate shame, can describe Brocklehurst's "sublime" sermon on her with cutting sarcasm and recalls that, even at the time, she surveyed the scene in the schoolroom with the amused detachment she had learned at Gateshead:

> Now came a pause of ten minutes, during which I—by this time in
> perfect possession of my wits—observed all the female Brockle-

hursts produce their pocket-handkerchiefs and apply them to their optics, while the elderly lady swayed herself to and fro, and the two younger ones whispered "How shocking!" (98–99)

From Jane's superior position on the stool the shocked Brocklehurst ladies look like a sea of silk and feathers, and Jane sees their ridiculousness. Her bird's-eye view alters her perspective psychologically, and she surprises herself by being so self-controlled: "I mastered the rising hysteria, lifted up my head, and took a firm stand on the stool" (99). Jane is metaphorically "propped up" by the sympathetic glances of other pupils: "How the new feeling bore me up! It was as if a martyr, a hero, had passed a slave or victim, and imparted strength in the transit" (99). But once left alone at the end of her own "martyrdom"— "nothing sustained me" (100)—Jane is literally as well as emotionally "knocked down" by the experience, "so overwhelming was the grief that seized me, I sank prostrate with my face to the ground . . . left to myself I abandoned myself" (100). Avowing to Helen that she would rather be the object of torture than of dislike (101), Jane is reproved for caring "too much of the love of human beings;" (101) and for relying solely on their approval: "If all the world hated you, and believed you wicked, while your own conscience approved you, and absolved you from guilt, you would not be without friends" (101), says Helen.

What Jane learns is that being dubbed a liar does not make her one, any more than Helen's wearing the placard of "Slattern" (105) makes it so. She learns that whatever Brocklehurst "might do with the outside of the cup and platter, the inside was farther beyond his interference than he imagined" (96): whatever label may be pinned on her, Jane's soul remains her own.

"The Work of My Own Hands"

As a direct consequence of being labeled a "Liar" Jane is declared innocent. To her surprise Jane's side of the story is readily believed by Miss Temple, and she is cleared "from every imputation" before the whole school. "Thus relieved of a grievous load" (106) of past guilt, her mental faculties are no longer preoccupied with self-comfort:

> That night, on going to bed, I forgot to prepare in imagination the Barmecide supper . . . with which I was wont to amuse my inward cravings. I feasted instead on the spectacle of ideal drawings, which I saw in the dark—all the work of my own hands. (106)

This is one of the most significant turning points in Jane's life: the personal sense of self-worth derived from the approval of the school enables her to be creative and curious. She works assiduously at her lessons, and, above all, she begins to paint: "In less than two months I was allowed to commence French and drawing. . . . sketched my first cottage (whose walls by the way outrivalled in slope those of the leaning tower of Pisa)" (106). Jane's previous wish-fulfillment fantasies switch from "hot roast potatoes" to "freely pencilled houses and trees, picturesque rocks and ruins, Cuyp-like groups of cattle, sweet paintings of butterflies hovering over unblown roses" (106).

At first Jane paints comfortable domestic scenes, but then she becomes increasingly adventurous, both artistically and physically: as she explores the horizons of Lowood she also explores the limits of her inner landscape. By the time she is eighteen, Jane has produced the strange visionary landscape paintings that we see in the next chapter, and she has also become dissatisfied with the limitations of her "views." Just as the safe harbor behind curtains at Gateshead had become intolerable, the protective "skirts" of Lowood seem "prison-ground, exile limits" (117), and Jane longs to travel further into what she sees in her mind's eye:

> My eye passed all other objects to rest on those most remote, the blue peaks. It was those I longed to surmount; all within their boundary of rock and heath seemed prison-ground, exile limits. I traced the white road winding round the base of one mountain, and

vanishing in a gorge between two. How I longed to follow it farther! (117)

Jane's landscape clearly is fashioned by her imagination. The psychic
excursion she undertakes eventually leads her, as Rochester propheti-
cally promises, to the "edge of a crater" (295), but the next important
stage of her journey is Thornfield.

THORNFIELD:
"FLOWERS AND THORNS"

When Jane arrives at Thornfield she feels that "a fairer era of life was beginning for me, one that was to have its flowers and pleasures as well as its thorns and toils" (130). Thornfield is, as its name suggests, the place of Jane's greatest trial and temptation, although it also sees the interrupted beginnings of her later happiness. When Jane arrives and is first shown through the intimidating mansion—where "a very chill and vault-like air pervaded the stairs and the gallery, suggesting cheerless ideas of space and solitude"—to the "safe haven" of her own room, it is emblematic of her metaphysical "journey" through Thornfield, to being truly "at home" with herself: "My couch had no thorns in it that night; my solitary room no fears" (129).

The Thornfield section opens with one of the most important self-portraits in the autobiography: the landscape paintings that Jane executed at Lowood but describes in detail while she shows them to Rochester—perhaps the only person who can understand them (he later employs their imagery to explain Jane to herself). Jane's surrealistic art (long before the genre had been thought of) uses landscape as the vehicle for a psychological drama, although its obvious inadequacy points to her later decision to become a writer, reminding us of Elizabeth Gaskell's comment on Brontë: "After she had tried to *draw* stories and not succeeded, she took the better mode of writing."[66]

The paintings reveal Jane's psychological as well as artistic limitations when she arrives at Thornfield: her bias is clearly romantic. Jane sees the world with the same intensely imaginative vision that had produced the nightmarish landscapes. Her lack of intellectual curiosity in the bizaare events that begin to occur makes her seem complicitous in her own harassment, and the alacrity with which she responds to the increasingly horrible occurrences suggests that she somehow expects them. Indeed, there is a sense in which this is true. Jane either imagines or dreams of all the important people at Thornfield—Mrs. Fairfax (126), Grace Poole (138), Rochester (143), and Bertha Mason (311)—before she actually meets them. With the last three she experiences a moment of recognition and implicit identity. At Thornfield, Jane's ability to distinguish between fantasy and reality almost breaks down, as the realistic illusion of the novel becomes increasingly strained (Bertha Mason's symbolic function, for example, threatens her credibility). The autobiographer begins, at Thornfield, the most daring and audacious exploration of her own mind, so that characters spring from increasingly remote regions.

Rochester, the most important person in Jane's life, is first encountered while she is exploring beyond the safe confines of Thornfield's garden, reminding us of Brontë's desire to take her heroine beyond the "cultivated garden" of realism. As the autobiographer describes the vicissitudes of her relationship with Rochester, she simultaneously flirts with the possibilities of her romantic imagination. Probing the farthest reaches of her own mind, the writer discovers Bertha Mason and recoils into the realistic mode that characterizes the following section. First, however, we pursue the young Jane into the innermost recesses of Thornfield manor, and Jane the autobiographer into her landscapes.

THE LANDSCAPES

If, as the autobiographer observes, "a new chapter in a novel is something like a new scene in a play" (125), then Jane's surrealistic landscapes are the backdrop, for not only do they indicate in general the romantic, even gothic, vision informing this section of the novel, they are individually significant enough to be described in detail to the reader. Rochester immediately recognizes them to be what Freud later called "dream work": "I dare say you did exist in a kind of artist's dream-land while you blent and arranged these strange tints" (158), and Jane confirms that "to paint them . . . was to enjoy one of the keenest pleasures I have ever known" (157). At Thornfield Jane seems unwilling to emerge from "the artist's dream-land" in which she has been wandering; if, as Rochester observes, she still carries the "Lowood restraint" about her, she also has its private indulgences. At Thornfield, indeed, reality begins to resemble her wildest fantasies (or is it the other way round?). If at Gateshead Jane was so influenced by her reading that she enacted the part of the "revolted slave" (46), at Thornfield she is a Gothic heroine, confined to a castlelike mansion (complete with battlements), with demonic laughter coming from the walls and a master who resembles a beast (though Jane is no beauty). Jane is extremely alive to the dramatic possibilities of her life: when wandering beyond Thornfield's grounds, in a contemplative state, she hears what she thinks is the "Gytrash" (147) of legend, but meets Rochester. She is also keenly aware, it seems, of the artistic possibilities: Rochester's face "was like a new picture introduced to the gallery of memory, and it was dissimilar to all the others hanging there" (147). At the age of eighteen Jane already has a strong visual imagination.

All three surrealistic landscapes represent an exploration of the bleaker regions of the mind that are intimidating and potentially dangerous; all have a solitary and isolated figure that seems formed out of the natural elements: they represent the three fundamental states of sinking, rising, and stasis; or drowning, being born, and being petrified. They indicate and concurrently dramatize a relationship with the subconscious self.

The first, which depicts a black cormorant (escaped perhaps from Bewick's book of birds [40]) snatching a gold bracelet from the arm of a girl drowning in a green swollen sea, with all else "in eclipse" (157), evokes the existential terror that Jane experienced when Helen

Burns was snatched from her and all she could see was an "unfathomed gulf" (110). The fact that there is no land symbolizes Jane's
inability to discover a solid ground of belief in herself, so that with
nothing to buoy her up she is terrified by the possibility of losing herself in her fantasies. The second picture of half a female figure rising
out of the hills into the sky represents a birth or a victorious resurrec-
tion, perhaps the birth of Jane's self at Lowood (an entirely feminine
environment) concurrently with the triumphant discovery of her creativity. The figure, with its hair streaming out "like a beamless cloud
torn by storm, or by electric travail" (157), is remarkably like Charlotte Brontë's childhood hero, "the Genius of the Storm," whom she
imagined as striding "over the black clouds which rolled beneath his
feet and regardless of the fierce lightning which flashed around him."[67]
This embodiment of Brontë's imagination was, throughout her life,
associated with the mixed excitement and fear aroused by a storm:
"Glorious! That blast was mighty. . . . Oh! it has awakened a feeling
that I cannot satisfy."[68] This second portrait seems to be a feminized
version of Brontë's "Genius of the Storm." In the preface to *Jane Eyre,*
Thackeray's genius is similarly described as an "electric death spark"
hidden in the "womb" of his creative mind (36).

If this portrait combines all the feminine forces in the novel, the
last epitomizes the masculine, seeming to be a combination of Rochester and St John. The rather exotic turban and sable veil anticipate
Rochester's appearance during charades, when Jane first acknowledges that she is in love with him (212). The figure has characteristics
common to Rochester and to St John, being harsh, unyielding, and
cold. It also, which is sinister, alludes to the figure of Death in *Paradise
Lost* (bk. 2, l. 666). All three portraits are partially obscured, as
though it were impossible for Jane to fully realize her conceptions:
"As I saw them with the spiritual eye, before I attempted to embody
them, they were striking; but my hand would not second my fancy,
and in each case it had wrought out but a pale portrait of the thing I
had conceived" (156–57).

Each painting is a momentary vision, fading even while glimpsed.
If Jane had possessed Freudian terminology, she could have explained

that these were revelations of her subconscious: like dreams they take elements from everyday life and distort them out of recognition. If they seem prophetic (as dreams often do) and can be linked to actual occurrences in the novel, this is because they express inner fears (and aspirations) for which we can always find confirmation in our lives. All three paintings indicate the desperate attempt to transcend circumstances that are potentially fatal. All three figures are presented amidst uncontrollable elemental forces: the first is threatened with drowning, and the last with petrifaction. Only the central female creative "Genius of the Storm" is victorious over the elements: she rises above the same blue peaks that Jane had glimpsed at Lowood. It is clear that if Jane allows herself to be overwhelmed by, or to submit to, her mental faculties, they could destroy her. The most ambiguous figure is the male, or androgynous portrait, which beneath its apparent grandeur dissolves into black clouds and shapelessness; the eyes are "hollow" and "blank of meaning, but for the glassiness of despair" (157). The words "hollow" and "glassiness" recall Jane's self-portrait in the red-room, and her childhood terror is repeated in the figure's petrification. Not surprisingly then, the picture anticipates the potential dangers of Jane's relationships with the two men in her life, both of whom, in their different ways, threaten to reduce her to her former bodilessness. But more important, the painting represents Jane's ambivalence toward her potent, yet perhaps illusory creative imagination.

ROCHESTER: JANE'S ROMANTIC GENIUS

This third "colossal head" (157), rising out of the elements, is remarkably reminiscent of Brontë's description of her sister Emily's hero Heathcliff: "From the crag . . . a head, savage, swart, sinister. . . . With time and labour, the crag took human shape; and there it stands colossal, dark, and frowning, half statue, half rock" (CH, 288). Rochester is very similarly described in *Jane Eyre* as having granite-hewn features: "colourless, olive face, square, massive brow, broad and jetty eyebrows, deep eyes, strong features, firm, grim mouth" (204). Even before Jane sees Rochester, as she hears him approach, a "solid mass of a crag" forms itself spontaneously in her mind as "in a picture" (143). Rochester, like Heathcliff, seems to spring directly from the natural elements of the mind. In the same passage in which she defends her sister's art, "wild and knotty as a root of heath," Charlotte Brontë compares the imagination to a sculptor who "sets to work on statue-hewing" (CH, 287) from the rocks of the mental landscape. The Brontë sisters' heroes, then, embody their own most potent mental powers. Whereas to the young Jane, Rochester is simply a Byronic hero, the mature autobiographer recognizes that there was something "in my brain and heart . . . that assimilates me mentally to him" (204): it would have been more accurate to reverse this, since Rochester is indeed a projection of something in Jane herself.

It is extremely significant that Jane meets Rochester beyond the walls of Thornfield, when she actually ventures into a region previously only glimpsed while pacing the attic lost in reverie:

> Then my sole relief was to walk along the corridor of the third story, backwards and forwards, safe in the silence and solitude of the spot, and allow my mind's eye to dwell on whatever bright visions rose before it. . . . and, best of all, to open my inward ear to a tale that was never ended—a tale my imagination created, and narrated continuously. (141)

As Jane's fantasies are becoming less static, increasingly narrative, they are less able to be realized on canvas and point toward the necessity of Jane's becoming a writer. (Indeed, Jane almost abandons painting at Thornfield, perhaps finding enough outlet for her fantasies in everyday life, not needing therefore to expend them on canvas.) At times of intense introspection in the attic at Thornfield, Jane "longed for a power of vision which might overpass that limit" (140). It is as though the further inward she penetrates the more impatient she becomes with her mental limitations; her anxious pacing is an external symptom of her inward exploration:

It is in vain to say human beings ought to be satisfied with tranquility: they must have action; and they will make it if they cannot find it. Millions are condemned to a stiller doom than mine, and millions are in silent revolt against their lot. Nobody knows how many rebellions besides political rebellions ferment in the masses of life which people earth. Women are supposed to be very calm generally: but women feel just as men feel: they need exercise for their faculties, and a field for their efforts as much as their brothers do; they suffer from too rigid a restraint, too absolute a stagnation, precisely as men would suffer. (141)

Frustrated with domestic "stagnation," Jane exercises her faculties. She meets Rochester while literally beyond the limits of her vision, while wandering in that region beyond Thornfield's, and Jane Austen's, garden. Brontë herself recognized that to travel beyond the boundaries of artistic convention required great courage:

Unless I can look beyond the greatest Masters, and study Nature herself, I have no right to paint. Unless I can have the courage to use the language of Truth in preference to the jargon of Conventionality, I ought to be silent.[69]

Many readers are amused by the fact that Jane insists on calling Rochester "master" even when she is engaged to be married to him. In her letters and journals Charlotte Brontë frequently uses the word "master" for the imagination: "When authors write best," she explains, "an influence seems to waken in them which becomes their master—which will have its own way."[70] Thus when Emily Brontë created Heathcliff she was "mastered" by her imagination:

Whether it is right or advisable to create beings like Heathcliff, I do not know: I scarcely think it is. But this I know; the writer who possesses the creative gift owns something of which he is not always master—something that at times strangely wills and works for itself. (CH, 287)

Whereas to paint was once, for Jane, "to enjoy one of the keenest pleasures I have ever known" (157), she now prefers "the pleasure of vexing and soothing" Rochester "by turns" (187). While the young Jane flirts with Rochester, the autobiographer flirts with her imagination. Both are experiencing the thrill of a struggle for "mastery": "on the extreme brink I liked well to try my skill" (187), Jane recalls. She likens meeting Rochester to coming across a chasm in her visionary landscape, "as if I had been wandering amongst volcanic-looking hills, and had suddenly felt the ground quiver, and seen it gape; . . . I longed only to dare—to divine it" (217).

Rochester represents then, the as yet unexplored region of Jane's mental territory, her unfathomed imagination, which arouses her desire to penetrate further inwards. Hence the otherwise very odd expression of Jane's envy for Blanche Ingram, who could "look into the abyss at her leisure, explore its secrets and analyse their nature" (217). Rochester, in turn, has an uncanny ability to penetrate Jane's mental landscape: "Reason sits firm . . . she will not let the feelings burst away and hurry her to wild chasms. . . . strong wind, earthquake-shock, and fire may pass by" (230). Rochester, as we shall see, does indeed provide the "earthquake-shock" in Jane's journey, which threatens to swallow up her path.

"VIEWLESS FETTERS"

As soon as Jane meets Rochester in the lane, he supplies some of the "incident, life, fire, feeling, that I desired and had not in my actual existence" (141), making her wish to prolong the adventure:

> When I came to the stile, I stopped a minute, looked round and listened, with an idea that a horse's hoofs might ring on the causeway again, and that a rider in a cloak, and a Gytrash-like Newfoundland dog, might be again apparent. (147)

Her brief excursion into fantasy makes Jane loath to return to reality, to recross the threshold into domesticity: "I did not like re-entering

Thornfield. To pass its threshold was to return to stagnation; . . . to slip again over my faculties the viewless fetters of a uniform and too still existence" (147). The pattern exactly repeats Jane's first escape from the "gray hollow" of her childhood fears at Gateshead:

> I lingered at the gates; I lingered on the lawn; I paced backwards and forwards on the pavement: the shutters of the glass door were closed; I could not see into the interior, and both my eyes and spirit seemed drawn from the gloomy house—from the gray hollow filled with rayless cells—as it appeared to me. (148)

Although Thornfield is significantly less "rayless" than Gateshead, because Jane has filled it with meaning and is herself more internally substantial, she nevertheless feels that returning to the confines of an ordered existence is tantamount to destroying her creative vision, her exploration beyond the "invisible boundary." She does not, however, return to "too rigid a restraint, too absolute a stagnation" (141), because her new intercourse with Rochester opens "to a mind unacquainted with the world, glimpses of its scenes and ways" (177). As one early reviewer noticed, Jane and Rochester "travel over each other's minds" in a "fearless original way" (CH, 72). "I had a keen delight in . . . following him in thought through the new regions he disclosed" (177). As her intimacy with this "imperious" and unattainable man increases, Jane feels "as if he were my relation rather than my master" (177), and the autobiographer is beginning to be at ease with the romantic possibilities of this central event in the novel.

Just before Jane surrenders to romanticism, to the illusion of being "a favorite with Mr. Rochester" (190), however, she pulls herself up short. Learning of the existence of the rumored bride-to-be, Blanche Ingram, Jane feels that she has been a "fantastic idiot" for mistaking "sweet lies" for "nectar," for feeding a "secret love" that can only "lead *ignis-fatuus-like* into miry wilds whence there is no extrication" (190). (Little does Jane know, at the time, how prophetic this is.) Before "crossing the Rubicon" into unexplored territory Jane endeavors "to bring back with a strict hand such as had been straying through imagination's boundless and trackless waste, into the safe fold of common sense" (190). Thus common sense is the "safe fold" out of which Jane's thoughts have dangerously strayed.

Fearing the "miry wilds" of her previous landscape-painting, Jane attempts, through her art, to change her perspective. She does this by producing two portraits, both indicative of the common-sense attitude that she is determined to adopt. Jane's new pictures are clearly a reaction to the landscapes and indicate her fear of her imaginative tendencies. If imagination is a romantic ideal, the self-portrait in chalk and the miniature of Blanche Ingram (whom she has not yet seen) represent different aspects of the eighteenth-century rationalist ideal of art: the one being strictly mimetic and the other constructed formulaically according to artistic rules. They are a conscious effort on Jane's part to reject the romantic phase inaugurated by her landscapes and to replace it with stern, moralistic didacticism:

> Listen, then, Jane Eyre, to your sentence: to-morrow, place the glass before you, and draw in chalk your own picture, faithfully, without softening one defect; omit no harsh line, smooth away no displeasing irregularity, write under it, "Portrait of a Governess, disconnected, poor, and plain." (190)

The lesson is reinforced with a contrasting ivory miniature of "the loveliest face" Jane can imagine, fulfilling the Greek ideal of beauty "august yet harmonious lineaments, the Grecian neck and bust; . . . 'Blanche an accomplished lady of rank' " (191). Jane is later surprised by the accuracy of her construction of Blanche Ingram, but the likeness is superficial: "she answered point for point, both to my picture and Mrs. Fairfax's description. The noble bust, the sloping shoulders . . . but . . . She laughed continually: her laugh was satirical, and so was the habitual expression of her arched and haughty lip" (201–2).

Though superficially Jane's portrait of Blanche Ingram answers "point for point" to her appearance, the "likeness" fails to capture the true spirit of its subject; fails, that is, to convey what Brontë called the life that "throbs full and fast beneath"; in the same way, Jane's unsparingly "accurate" self-portrait fails to reveal the passion beneath. Although it is not until nearly the end of the novel that Jane discovers she has been, in actuality, neither "disconnected, poor," nor "plain," it is evident that this self-portrait is, like the preface to the autobiography, replete with false modesty: is in fact a parody, being an exaggerated application of eighteenth-century mimeticism. Each portrait then, because of its superficial accuracy, contains its own indictment, because the true spirit of each subject, what lies beneath her appearance, is the very opposite of what it seems.

The ivory miniature brings to mind Jane Austen's description of her own art as "a little bit (two Inches wide) of Ivory."[71] The style in this section of the novel is strongly reminiscent of Jane Austen's satire. With merciless unsympathetic accuracy Jane describes and passes judgment on the guests at Thornfield. The manner of presentation in the prose echoes that of the portraits—Rochester, disguised as a gypsy, is uncannily accurate about both Jane's private attitude and the effect of her "objectivity," which, in its dispassionate accuracy, deprives the characters of their humanity. Her lack of "sympathetic communion" makes them "mere shadows of human forms" (227), he says in an implicit indictment of mimeticism.

Although Jane congratulates herself on "the course of wholesome discipline to which I had thus forced my feelings to submit" (191), her dispassion makes her alienated, even embittered: "Genius is said to be self-conscious: I cannot tell whether Miss Ingram was a genius, but she was self-conscious—remarkably self-conscious indeed" (202). This section, which is often thought rather weak, is intended to show that Jane's own self-consciousness is not "genius." Her refusal to join the guests is as much due to her secret feelings of superiority as it is to her shyness. Hiding behind the "double retirement" of the curtains and her mask of humility, just as she had done at Gateshead, it is as though one of Jane's picture books has sprung to life before her eyes, but instead of *Bewick* we have a satirical comedy of manners. Jane is mercilessly critical of the futility and fatuousness of the Thornfield guests, yet acutely sensitive to anything they say that touches on herself; she is almost as "self-conscious" as Blanche, who is, in many respects, another of Jane's doubles—a combination, though exaggerated, of all that Jane aspires to at this time: she is proud, self-possessed, talented, and above all, flirtatious with Rochester (216). Jane, who is battling to suffocate feelings of love for Rochester, is painfully jealous. She is convinced (despite the show of humility) that she would be better for her "master" than the proud, frigid (bloodless and colorless as her name suggests) Blanche.

We have then in this section the rejection of Jane's habitual romantic mode combined with merciless satire; in retrospect the autobiographer recognizes that her vision of the Thornfield guests was symptomatic of Jane's efforts to reject love and compassion, and could only have been a temporary phase in her art: "Feeling without judgment is a washy draught indeed; but judgment untempered by feeling is too bitter and husky a morsel for human deglutition" (265). The pattern of Jane's combined emotional and artistic response to early events at Thornfield is an emblem of the development of the book as a whole. Jane had become so caught up in her fantasies of a romantic (in the popular sense) affair with her employer that she had, in her opinion, become blind to reality, had "rejected the real, and rapidly devoured the ideal" (190). She sees this as a failure of vision: "He said something in praise of your eyes, did he? Blind puppy! Open their bleared lids and look on your own accursed senselessness!" (190). But her attempt to control her own imagination by adopting the other extreme is soon shown to be equally misguided. It is Rochester, disguised as an ancient female bard or teller of fortunes, who prompts Jane's return to her more natural romanticism. We will see, however, that because of her continuing fears, it is still a "region of doubts and portents and dark conjectures" (194).

THE ORACLE

One of the first "portents" that Jane encounters is Rochester, disguised as an old witch, who tells her that her denial of imagination is making her "cold . . . sick, . . . and silly" (226). The oracle warns Jane that though she thinks she is being objective, her vision is as far removed from reality as if she were a prisoner in Plato's cave watching shadows on the wall. The criticism is as much of Jane's portraits, or her current aesthetic ideals, as it is of her personal attitude:

> "You sit in yonder room with the fine people flitting before you like shapes in a magic-lantern: just as little sympathetic communion passing between you and them as if they were really mere shadows of human forms, and not the actual substance." (227)

As if seeing into Jane's soul, the gypsy tells her that in her present mood she inhabits the ice-bound regions of her third landscape painting; she is resigned to a feelingless universe simply because she will not admit to her aspirations:

> "You are cold, because you are alone: no contact strikes the fire from you that is in you. You are sick, because the best of feelings, the highest and sweetest given to man, keeps far away from you. You are silly, because, suffer as you may, you will not beckon it to approach, nor will you stir one step to meet it where it waits for you." (226)

Although this is Rochester's cunning strategy for prompting Jane to admit that she is in love with him, it is also an extreme indictment of the common-sense view that Jane has been struggling to maintain. The gypsy's ability to read Jane's thoughts is so uncanny that her

> strange talk, voice, manner, had by this time wrapped me in a kind of dream. One unexpected sentence came from her lips after another, till I got involved in a web of mystification; and wondered what unseen spirit had been sitting for weeks by my heart watching its workings and taking record of every pulse. (228)

With the words of the oracle Jane begins to return to the imaginative dreamworld in which she had produced the landscapes. The unseen spirit at her heart, the oracle who tells Jane more about herself than she had been prepared to acknowledge, turns out to be not only Rochester but also a "double," another mirror image of her inner self. In the red-room Jane had seen herself, and now, beneath the red cloak, she sees a face as "familiar to me as my own face in a glass—as the speech of my own tongue" (231). It is not surprising then that the gypsy has a truly Freudian "uncanny" ability to tell Jane what she already knows.

NOW IN FIRE AND NOW IN BLOOD

When Rochester, in a female role, describes Jane's "desires" and "passions" as "strong wind, earthquake-shock, and fire" (230), he uses the images advisedly, not only because they are taken from Jane's paintings, but because at least one has already become a reality. Some nights before Jane's interview with the gypsy fortune-teller, she had been aroused in the night by "Grace Poole's" laughter to find smoke issuing from beneath Rochester's door. She rushes into his room in time to put out his flaming bed: "brought my own water-jug, baptized the couch afresh, and, by God's aid, succeeded in extinguishing the flames which were devouring it" (180). This is frequently regarded as a symbol for the onset of sexual attraction between Jane and Rochester, especially since he seems, after a near avowal of love, to expect her to stay, but she, having "cold feet" (and appropriately having just thrown cold water over his flames), returns to her room, to experience instead being "tossed on a buoyant but unquiet sea, where billows of trouble rolled under surges of joy" (182).

At Gateshead Jane had said that a devouring fire would be an apt symbol for her angry state of mind (69), but at Thornfield her anger seems to become a reality as she loses control over it. As Jane becomes increasingly unable to distinguish between inner and outer landscapes, what were previously metaphors take on a dramatic life of their own. It is the oracle who recognizes, more astutely than Jane, that what she takes to be an external agitation is actually inside herself. When the gypsy reminds Jane of the painful, unrequited love that she has been struggling to repress, she is so agitated that she complains of feeling "burned": "Don't keep me long; the fire scorches me" (229), and the oracle replies that the fire is in *her*: "The flame flickers in the eye" (229). In advising Jane to submit to her passions and her imagination, the oracle declares, "No contact strikes the fire from you that is in you" (226), and urges her to go forward to meet her desires rather than thwart them. The ideal is characteristically romantic, having aesthetic as well as personal implications. The romantics regarded the artist, and indeed every individual, as "a lamp" (to use M. H. Abrams's famous analogy) that illuminates reality—confers meaning and life on an otherwise inanimate universe.[72] Rochester, disguised as an oracle who seems to Jane to be the very spirit within her, declares Jane is indeed capable of realizing her fantasies, of creating her own reality. The gypsy's voice seems to be that of Jane's own romantic aspirations. Soon after this Jane's art again changes abruptly, and, without willing it, she reverts to an extremely romantic style: that of the direct transcription of her imagination without any mediating consciousness. During the interview with the fortune-teller Jane seems to be falling under the spell of a powerful force, so that she cannot tell whether or not she is awake: "Where was I? Did I wake or sleep? Had I been dreaming?" (231).

Jane's willingness to be drawn into Rochester's "web of mystification" (228) initiates a series of events that are indeed more like dream, or nightmare, than reality, and Jane begins to feel that she is playing a part in a melodrama. There is a strong sense of Jane's self-dramatization in this section, created by explicit allusions to plays and acting. Rochester's "masquerade," as Jane calls it (231), is punctuated with references to *Hamlet* (230) and *King Lear* (231), rather sinister for a game, and the charades played by the guests offer Jane, as we shall see, a reflection of her own potential folly. The explicitly dramatic nature of events at Thornfield prepares us to see all the characters surrounding Jane as Rochester claims they are, figures, even puppets, projected by the "magic lantern" (227) of Jane's own romantic mind, acting out before her eyes her deepest fears.

No wonder Jane begins to ask what was the "mystery, that broke out, now in fire and now in blood?" (239), but her questions imply the answer: "What crime was this, that lived incarnate in this sequestered mansion?" (239). The fire in Rochester's bedroom is followed by a brutal attack on Mr. Mason in the night. Jane immediately knows that she is "wanted" when she hears "the voice I expected to hear, namely, my master's" (237), and she is left in charge of the maimed victim while Rochester goes for a doctor.

Once again Jane is locked in an antique bedroom, watching reflections, which this time change with "the shifting obscurity and flickering gleam" of shapes that seem to grow out of the panels (239), and once again she admits that "my own thoughts worried me." But now, instead of seeing a fairy or an imp, she is threatened with "a revelation of the arch-traitor—of Satan himself—in his subordinate's form" (239). The "form," however, is feminine. "What creature was it, that, masked in an ordinary woman's face and shape, uttered the voice, now of a mocking demon, and anon of a carrion-seeking bird of prey?" (239–40). Jane still carries around in her head the figures from Bewick's *History of British Birds* with which she once identified.

Jane's fears are clearly now more substantial: instead of being afraid that "a ghost would come" (49), she is "afraid of someone coming out of the inner room" (245):

> Here, then, was I in the third story, fastened into one of its mystic cells; night around me; a pale and bloody spectacle under my eyes and hands; a murderess hardly separated from me by a single door: yes—that was appalling—the rest I could bear; but I shuddered at the thought of Grace Poole bursting out upon me. (239)

Nothing does burst out, because Rochester guards the key. Not until Jane surrenders to her romantic "master" does she penetrate to the inaccessible regions of her inner and outer landscapes.

THE AUTOMATIC PORTRAIT

As though to retrieve her sense of self after this frightening near-revelation, Jane goes back to the scene of her past crisis of identity.

She answers a summons from her dying Aunt Reed and returns to Gateshead, perhaps sensing that in order to progress she must first travel backward. "I still felt as a wanderer on the face of the earth," she observes, "but I experienced firmer trust in myself and my own powers, and less withering dread of oppression." (256).

It is usually suggested that Jane is prompted by Helen Burns's example to forgive Mrs. Reed for the injustices of the past, but the position of the event in the novel suggests otherwise. It seems that whatever malignant force had threatened Rochester (with fire) and Mason (with blood) has shocked Jane into a recognition of the potential effects of resentment, and the need for forgiveness.

At her aunt's, Jane is willing to affirm and practice the "sympathetic communion" urged by the oracle: "The gaping wound of my wrongs, too, was now quite healed; and the flame of resentment extinguished" (256). It was Jane herself who extinguished the flames. She forgives and even sympathizes with one who had been utterly inimical to her. It coincides with a radical change in her artistic practice, a return to the most extreme expression of her imagination.

Sitting in the window seat at Gateshead as she had done long ago, Jane reverts to the former romantic-expressionism of her landscape paintings:

> Provided with a case of pencils, and some sheets of paper, I used to take a seat apart from them, near the window, and busy myself in sketching fancy vignettes representing any scene that happened momentarily to shape itself in the ever-shifting kaleidoscope of imagination: a glimpse of sea between two rocks; the rising moon, and a ship crossing its disc; a group of reeds and water-flags, and a naiad's head, crowned with lotus-flowers, rising out of them; an elf sitting in a hedge-sparrow's nest, under a wreath of hawthorn bloom. (261)

This is a combination of the early studies from nature and the later fantasy art, though greatly softened. In place of the Medusa-like head of the second landscape we have a naiad's crowned in flowers of love: this is an enchanted fairy world; like Titania, Jane is bewitched.

Suddenly, without willing it, Jane finds a portrait forming itself beneath her hand:

> One morning I fell to sketching a face: what sort of face it was to be, I did not care or know. I took a soft black pencil, gave it a broad point, and worked away. Soon I had traced on the paper a broad and prominent forehead and a square lower outline of visage: that contour gave me pleasure; my fingers proceeded actively to fill it with features. Strong-marked horizontal eyebrows must be traced under that brow. (261)

The image is Rochester as a rough and rugged hunk of rock, "a decided cleft" in his firm chin, and "jetty hair" (262). What is significant about this latest portrait is that it represents the most extreme form that romanticism can take: being, like automatic writing, entirely unmediated by conscious deliberation. Jane wants to do full justice to the romantic spirit of her subject: "I surveyed the effect: 'they want more force and spirit!'; and I wrought the shades blacker, that the lights might flash more brilliantly" (262). To Jane the face is more real than those of the people around her: "There, I had a friend's face under my gaze: and what did it signify that those young ladies turned their backs on me?" (262). Jane has clearly given herself up to her "master," surrendering her powers of judgment and throwing off the restraints of her rational mind in favor of following up the inclinations of her imagination. As she does so, the imaginary "ideal" conception that she has of Rochester becomes more real to her than the objective external world. She is, clearly, unwilling to extricate herself from his "web of mystification." From now until her near-union with Rochester, Jane becomes increasingly unable to distinguish between fantasy and reality.

ROCHESTER'S AUTOBIOGRAPHY

In this mood of surrender Jane returns to Thornfield; it seems she had secretly longed for the advice offered by the gypsy to "beckon" to her "highest and sweetest aspirations." When she first sees Rochester again (this time it is Jane who approaches unobserved), he is not reading (like Helen Burns, Diana, and Mary) but "sitting there, a book and pencil in his hand; he is writing" (272). Jane is reminded of their original meeting: did she doubt the reality of her idol?: "Well, he is not a ghost: yet every nerve I have is unstrung: for a moment I am beyond my own mastery. What does it mean?" (272). It means that Jane has been "mastered" by her romantic imagination.

Rochester, who "puts up his book and his pencil" (272) almost surreptitiously when he sees Jane, is, significantly, engaged in writing his own autobiography, which (we later learn) casts Jane as a good angel who will clear him from past guilt and make all his dreams come true. Rochester, absorbed in his fairy-tale world, greets Jane accordingly: "If I dared, I'd touch you to see if you are substance or shadow, you elf! but I'd as soon offer to take hold of a blue *ignis fatuus* light in a marsh" (272–73). Rochester unwittingly alludes not only to Jane's wraithlike appearance in the mirror at Gateshead but also to her own earlier fear that she too was pursuing an "ignis fatuus" into "miry wilds whence there is no extrication"; neither can foresee the end of the journey on which they have embarked. Rochester's next words do threaten to turn Jane back into the mere specter that she was at Gateshead. When he tells her that he is to marry Blanche Ingram and has found her a position with "Mrs. O'Gall" of "Bitternut Lodge" (279) (Jane misses the innuendos), Jane feels as though the new foundations on which she had begun to build a sense of herself are being torn down. For the first time in her life she had experienced the pleasures of being with someone who felt like a relation, and both her body and soul had expanded ("I gathered flesh and strength" [177]). But now Rochester threatens to cancel her out again, as though she were inconsequential; roused to what she calls, in an understatement, "something like passion," Jane rebels as daringly as she had at Gateshead, but with the eloquence of increased self-confidence: "The vehemence of emotion, stirred by grief and love within me, was claiming mastery, and struggling for full sway, and asserting a right to predominate, to overcome, to live, rise, and reign at last: yes—and to speak" (280–81).

What Jane says is an absolute denial of her previous portrait of herself as "disconnected, poor, plain." She now recognizes that although she does not have Blanche Ingram's external attributes, she has something of much greater value "beneath the surface," the passion that "throbs full and fast":

> Do you think I can stay to become nothing to you? Do you think I am an automaton?—a machine without feelings? . . . Do you think, because I am poor, obscure, plain, and little, I am soulless and heartless? You think wrong!—I have as much soul as you—and full as much heart! And if God had gifted me with some beauty and much wealth, I should have made it as hard for you to leave me, as it is now for me to leave you. I am not talking to you now through the medium of custom, conventionalities, nor even of mortal flesh: it is my spirit that addresses your spirit; just as if both had passed through the grave, and we stood at God's feet, equal—as we are! (281)

Jane's declaration of equality despite gender and class differences offended many Victorian readers, but she is following the advice of the oracle and beckoning very decidedly to her good fortune; as if to confirm it, Rochester immediately proposes marriage. Jane, not surprisingly, seeks evidence of his sincerity and asks to "read" his countenance. Rochester, who has recently been writing his autobiography, finds an analogy immediately: "You will find it scarcely more legible than a crumpled, scratched page. Read on: only make haste, for I suffer" (283) Jane, however, misses the ambiguity of Rochester's "suffering" and fails to inquire too closely into the reasons for it: fails, that is, to read between the lines. Jane is only too willing to corroborate Rochester's story and to join him in his fantasy.

When Rochester tells little Adèle the fairy tale of his romance with Jane, however, she is a much less credulous listener than her governess:

> I sat down to rest me on a stile; and there I took out a little book and a pencil, and began to write about a misfortune that befell me

long ago, and a wish I had for happy days to come. I was writing away very fast, though daylight was fading from the leaf, when something came up the path and stopped two yards off me. . . . It was a fairy, and come from Elf-land, it said; and its errand was to make me happy! (295–96)

When Rochester proposes to place Jane at the "edge of a crater" in one of her visionary landscapes, he is unaware just how prophetic that will be:

I am to take mademoiselle to the moon, and there I shall seek a cave in one of the white valleys among the volcano-tops, and mademoi-selle shall live with me there, and only me. . . . Fire rises out of the lunar mountains: when she is cold I'll carry her up to a peak, and lay her down on the edge of a crater. (295)

Adèle's skepticism is more accurate than Rochester's extravagance: "there is no road to the moon; it is all air; and neither you nor she can fly" (295). Jane is soon to discover how right is Adèle's common-sense observation that there are no roads to the moon.

THE OTHER SIDE OF THE STORY

All her life Jane has been undervalued and mistreated, but at Thornfield she tells Rochester: "I have not been trampled on. I have not been petrified. I have not been buried with inferior minds" (281). Quite rightly she wishes to be prized for herself alone, and not for any purpose she may serve. Although Jane longs to make this fairy-tale romance into a reality, she discovers that her version does not quite coincide with Rochester's. When he declares his intention to "clasp the bracelets on these fine wrists, and load these fairy-like fingers with rings" (287), Jane retorts, "Don't address me as if I were a beauty; I am your plain, Quakerish governess" (287). Whenever Rochester begins to romanticize: "I will attire my Jane in satin and lace, and she shall have roses in her hair; and I will cover the head I love best with a priceless veil" (288), Jane brings him back to earth: "and I shall not be your Jane Eyre any longer, but an ape in a harlequin's jacket—a jay in borrowed plumes" (288). The debate is of course about something much more fundamental than appearance. Jane has heard the long story of Céline Varens and Rochester's other failed love affairs, and she suspects that he is attempting to dress her like another mistress in his private drama: "I'll wear nothing but my old Lowood frocks to the end of the chapter" (297), Jane remarks, referring rather caustically to their "story"; Rochester reacts to this as though it were just another kind of charade: "Is she original? Is she piquant? I would not exchange this one little English girl for the Grand Turk's whole seraglio–gazelle-eyes, houri forms, and all!" (297). Jane is being written into Rochester's own life story as the last in the line of mistresses—the love affair that will be a success and change everything. She suspects, without consciously acknowledging it, that Rochester wishes to use her as an instrument of his salvation: "wherever I stamped my hoof, your sylph's foot shall step also" (288). Rochester is simply expressing the prevalent Victorian belief that woman is an "Angel in the House" (the title of Coventry Patmore's best-selling narrative poem of marital love) whose innocence and virtue act as an antidote to the corrupting effects of man's necessary dealings with the world. Rochester wants Jane to be a leisured middle-class wife (one who remains aloof from the "business" of life), but she resists both his suggestion that she give up being a governess and his gifts; she does not react to the jewels and gowns in the way a good heroine should: "Glad was I to get him out of the silk warehouse, and then out of a jeweller's shop: the more he bought me, the more my cheek burned with a sense of annoyance and degradation" (297).

Jane resents that her own identity is being taken away—"I never can bear being dressed like a doll by Mr. Rochester" (297)—and that in Rochester's private drama she is a fairy, a sylph, an angel, an elf: always a romanticized figure, never herself. When Rochester reflects: "Ten years since, I flew through Europe half mad: with disgust, hate, and rage as my companions; now I shall revisit it healed and cleansed, with a very angel as my comforter" (288), Jane replies archly that he "must neither expect nor exact anything celestial of me" (288).

Jane is clearly resisting romantic idealization, but she recalls that Rochester "pursued his theme . . . without noticing my deprecation" (288); because she wishes very much to become Mrs. Rochester, Jane attempts to repress her ambivalent feelings. The mutual raillery between Jane and Rochester, though an expression of their exhilaration in one another's company, has perplexing undertones. When Jane asks to have her curiosity satisfied over a burning question, Rochester's wish that she would resist her desire for knowledge is no mere jest: "Don't long for poison—don't turn out a downright Eve on my hands!" (290). In Rochester's mythologizing, Jane is either the angel or the whore: responsible either for his salvation or his downfall. Jane is oblivious to the real cause for Rochester's fear; she will not "read between the lines" of his evident agitation.

The most important of the costumes in which Rochester attempts to dress Jane is the wedding veil. Unable to believe in the identity that it signifies, Jane immediately on receiving the veil locks it in the closet:

> Mrs. Rochester! She did not exist: she would not be born till to-morrow. . . . It was enough that in yonder closet . . . garments said to be hers had already displaced my black stuff Lowood frock and straw bonnet. . . . I shut the door to conceal the strange, wraith-like apparel it contained which . . . gave out certainly a most ghostly shimmer through the shadow of my apartment. (303)

The intense irony with which these words are charged is of course not apparent until we later discover that there is in fact a Mrs. Rochester already in existence, who has already threatened to burst out of the closet, and that it is *her* ghostly presence that haunts Jane's apartment. Even without the benefit of hindsight, however, the reader recognizes in this insubstantial "wraith" a repetition of Jane's apparition in the mirror at Gateshead. It is as though she has lost sight of herself—"My future husband was becoming to me my whole world" (302)—and cannot therefore believe in her future identity.

Jane's fear of what lies "in yonder closet" is actually a fear of what lies beneath her own apparent acquiescence in her marriage: ever since returning to Thornfield Jane has worn her own "veil":

> and solicitous only to appear calm; and, above all, to control the working muscles of my face—which I feel rebel insolently against my will, and struggle to express what I had resolved to conceal. But I have a veil—it is down: I may make shift yet to behave with decent composure. (272)

The veil is, however, to be torn before long, and Jane is to be stripped of her illusions. When she tells Rochester that she regards the expensive wedding veil he gives her as a symbol of his "pride," she is nevertheless undaunted "because I am used to the sight of the demon" (309), but she is as yet unacquainted with her own demon, her similar indomitable pride that secretly resents being used as the instrument of Rochester's salvation and that causes her to make the rather paradoxical comment on her future wedding: "There was no putting off the day that advanced" (303).

"IN PERIL"

During the period leading up to her marriage Jane is unusually and inexplicably apprehensive. Her love for Rochester eclipses all else, including her sense of self:

> My future husband was becoming to me my whole world; and more than the world; almost my hope of heaven. He stood between me and every thought of religion, as an eclipse intervenes between man and the broad sun. I could not, in those days, see God for His creature: of whom I had made an idol. (302)

Jane is uneasy because she senses that beneath the incredible allure of Rochester's romantic picture of their life together is something false. She suspects that his dream is just that, making everything insubstantial. She tells Rochester that "Everything in life seems unreal" and "you sir, are the most phantom-like of all: you are a mere dream" (306–7).

Rochester, the autobiographer's embodiment of romanticism, thus stands between Jane and God, Jane and the world. This section of the novel consequently blurs the division between fantasy and reality: as Jane is overcome by Rochester, the autobiographer is overpowered by her imagination. Whereas in the earlier sections of the autobiography, the landscape and weather represent Jane's inner self, here the process is reversed: it is nature that somehow takes the initiative and actively communicates with Jane's subconscious. Jane becomes wholly attuned to the other-worldly and takes very seriously the messages from omens, dreams, and presentiments, believing firmly in "the sympathies of Nature with man" (249). Thus when the chestnut tree under which Rochester proposed marriage is burned and riven by lightning, Jane addresses the two halves as if they were indeed a human pair like herself and Rochester:

> "You did right to hold fast to each other," I said: as if the monster splinters were living things, and could hear me. "I think, scathed as you look, and charred and scorched, there must be a little sense of life in you yet . . . each of you has a comrade to sympathize with him in his decay." (304)

Rochester, though in jest, recognizes Jane's ability to slip backwards and forwards across the physical and spiritual boundaries: "'I have been with my aunt sir, who is dead.' 'A true Janian reply! . . . She comes from the other world—from the abode of people who are dead!'" (272). When Rochester asks Jane whether she is "apprehensive of the new sphere you are about to enter?" (307), she replies that she is not, but her dreams suggest otherwise. John Keats once compared the romantic imagination to "Adam's dream—he awoke and found it Truth."[73] Jane is about to experience this same sensation. She finds that her dreams come true, in a way that she does not expect. The night preceding her wedding eve Jane is bewildered by two dreams, one of which she suspects is an apparition. The first is a recurrence of the nightmares she had for a week before her aunt died, of a little child who this time "clung round my neck in terror, and almost strangled me" (310). In the dream Rochester is departing in the same manner as he had come into Jane's life—on horseback. On Jane's wedding morning, the child is uncannily realized in Adèle, to whom Jane would otherwise be overreacting:

> I remember Adèle clung to me as I left her: I remember I kissed her as I loosened her little hands from my neck; and I cried over her with strange emotion, and quitted her because I feared my sobs would break her still sound repose. She seemed the emblem of my past life. (314)

If Adèle is an "emblem" of Jane's past, Rochester, she says, is "the dread, but adored, *type* of my unknown future day" (314, emphasis mine). Victorian readers would have immediately understood something very different and specific by the word "type" that is lost to us today. Imbued as they were with typological interpretations of the Scriptures, they would have recognized that by calling Rochester the "type" of her future, Jane intends his significance to extend beyond his ordinary self. Like all scriptural characters in the eyes of the Victorians, Rochester as a "type" of Jane's self is intended to embody a moral and spiritual lesson. But in order to learn it Jane must first recognize that the characters she finds less attractive than her "master" are also "emblems" of her own state.

GRACE POOLE

Although Jane feels "akin" to Rochester and therefore understands "the language of his countenance and movements" (204), she is unable to interpret the enigmatic Grace Poole. At first sight the "commonplace features," devoid of emotion, bear little resemblance to Jane's, but Grace, the most ambiguous character in the autobiography, embodies Jane's inner contradictions and her unacknowledged ambivalence toward her own situation. What perplexes and fascinates Jane about Grace Poole is the disparity between her appearance and the "malignant pranks" (185) for which she is apparently responsible.

When Jane is told that the mirthless laughter that echoes through Thornfield is the housemaid's (139), she is surprised: "any apparition less romantic or less ghostly could scarcely be conceived" (138). Grace Poole's "appearance always acted as a damper to the curiosity raised by her oral oddities" (142): "There she sat, staid and taciturn-looking, as usual, in her brown stiff gown, her check apron, white hankerchief, and cap. She was intent on her work, in which her whole thoughts seemed absorbed" (183). This vacant creature who spends her time sewing is the epitome of those women whom Jane describes as suffering from "too rigid a restraint, too absolute a stagnation" by being confined to "making puddings and knitting stockings, to playing on the piano and embroidering bags" (141). When Charlotte Brontë was herself a governess, she wrote to her friend Ellen Nussey that she was expected "to do a good deal of sewing" and that the necessity of suppressing her creativity made her sick: "It is . . .—the estrangement from one's real character—the adoption of a cold, rigid, apathetic exterior, that is painful" (L, 217).

Grace Poole is therefore the paradigm of self-estrangement: the "cold, rigid, apathetic, exterior" of a typical Victorian woman is also the source of "demoniac" laughter (179), "eccentric murmurs" (141), and even "attempted murder" (183). She is, then, one of the "millions" of women with whom Jane identifies while pacing in the attic, who like herself is "in silent revolt against their lot" (141).

Whenever Jane longs to break through the restraints of her domestic existence, she hears what she takes to be Grace Poole's laughter, though this is of course an illusory explanation. What is interesting about Jane's attempt to decipher the "language" of Grace Poole's "countenance and movements" is the readiness with which she accepts that this is an ordinary woman who harbors murderous desires. Jane seems to understand Grace so well that she thinks she can beat her at her own game: "Fiend! she wants to know my habits, so that she may lay her plans accordingly!" (185).

It is Grace Poole who advises Jane to "have a drawn bolt between one and any mischief that may be about" (185), thus protecting Jane from the knowledge of Bertha Mason; she is in a sense the "grace" by which Jane is protected from herself, the screen behind which anger rages. Since Jane's angry, passionate, emotions are represented by fire, Mrs. Poole is appropriately named as the "damper" to Jane's agitation. When Jane puts out the fire that almost destroys Rochester, he observes that she is "Cold . . . and standing in a pool!" (182).

There is, then, a great deal of evidence to suggest that Grace Poole, the "square-made figure . . . with a hard, plain face" (138), is a visual emblem of Jane's own self-suppression.

BERTHA MASON

Hiding behind Grace Poole's masklike visage is Bertha Mason. It was she, Jane learns, who almost burst out of the "great cabinet" in the third-story room in which Jane was "fastened" as if in a "mystic cell" (239), and it is she who is locked in Jane's own closet with the wedding veil (303). The interior furnishings of Thornfield manor suggest that they are objective correlatives of Jane's mind. When Jane arrived at Thornfield Rochester asked whether she had "furniture" within of the same kind as her paintings (156), thus establishing an identity between her inner and outer worlds. When Jane fancies saintly and demonic faces in the polished wood panels of the cupboard (289), it is a reflection of her own fears; whenever she paces in the attic, longing for a metaphysical power of vision, she hears weird laughter from behind the walls. It is difficult to tell whether the emanations are from the house or her own mind. As Jane, in the days leading up to her marriage, increasingly loses touch with the outside world, her "artist's dream-land" (158) becomes "a region of doubts and portents and dark conjectures" (194). The closer Jane is to union with Rochester, the more Bertha Mason makes herself known, finally emerging from Jane's closet to issue a warning.

Jane first sees Bertha's face in the mirror, and, as if to underline the point, her head is superimposed over Jane's own: "her lurid visage flamed over mine" (312). Bertha is clearly one of Jane's most important self-portraits, but the one she is least able to recognize. She is the most shocking of Jane's self-revelations and therefore the "double" that is most fully integrated into the narrative events. The two occasions on which Bertha manifests herself are clearly linked to Jane's past "epiphanies" of self-revelation. On the first occasion, Jane tells Rochester, she was so terrified of what she saw that she lost consciousness "for the second time in my life—only the second time" (312), thus deliberately recalling the red-room incident in which she also became "insensible from terror" of herself. This new mirror image, however, replaces the "white face" and "glittering eyes" (46) of fear and impotence with the flaming eyes and vividly exaggerated features of aggression and furious energy: "I wish I could forget the roll of the red eyes and the fearful blackened inflation of the lineaments!" (311). Bertha Mason is regarded quite rightly by Gilbert and Gubar in *The Madwoman in the Attic* as Jane's "truest and darkest double," the manifestation of her "hunger, rebellion, and rage,"[74] but Bertha's symbolic role is specific. Her destructive frustration is the result of being denied a creative "outlet." Her appearance is a distorted version of the female creative genius depicted in Jane's second painting, with her "dark and wild" eyes, streaming hair, and a form dissolving into shadow amidst "electric travail" (157). Bertha represents the reproductive powers of the imagination: her huge stature and "virile force" (321) are evidence of a strength and potency that is almost masculine. Rochester suggests that Bertha's insanity originated in a tendency to be "intemperate and unchaste" (334) and that her madness is a lack of control over language: "no professed harlot ever had a fouler vocabulary than she" (335). Furthermore, her setting light to the bed, and finally to Thornfield itself, is an exaggerated version of the romantic idea of the artist as a lamp illuminating reality; Bertha's energy literally ignites all around it. She represents for Jane, then, the dangers of extreme romanticism, of the inner self as the source of "reality." She is, as Rochester points out, "the creature of an over-stimulated brain" (312).

Perhaps the most important clue to the metaphorical significance of Bertha Mason is the fact that she wears, and then ritualistically tears, Jane's veil. Charlotte Brontë herself once likened the loss of illusion to the removal of a veil:

> I have now outlived youth; and, though I dare not say that I have outlived all its illusions—that the romance is quite gone from life—the veil fallen from truth, and that I see both in naked reality—yet, certainly, many things are not what they ten years ago. (L, 341)

Bertha Mason tears the veil and destroys Jane's illusory romance with Rochester. It is she who shows Jane the danger of losing touch with reality, of inhabiting a world of fantasy. Charlotte Brontë once became terrified by the products of her own introspection, declaring that her imagination "showed almost in the vivid light of reality the ongoings of the infernal world."[75] The revelation made her attempt to stop writing, and fantasizing, altogether; but she confessed to Ellen Nussey that the more she tried to suppress urges that few could understand, they would only "sting the deeper for concealment" and "rankle there like venom" until they "burst out sometimes, and then those who see the explosion despise me, and I hate myself for days afterwards" (L, 164). Bertha Mason is clearly an embodiment of this repressed creative urge, which "rankles" and finally "bursts out" furiously; she represents Brontë's fear that the imagination may be "a frenzy—a disease rather than a gift of the mind."[76] Bertha Mason, whose name recalls Brontë's personification of the imagination as a sculptor,[77] shows that creative genius is a very mixed blessing.

When Jane confronts Bertha, Rochester describes her standing "so grave and quiet at the mouth of hell, looking collectedly at the gambols of a demon" (322), which is remarkably like Brontë's confrontation of the "infernal world" in her own imagination. Jane once expressed a longing to explore "the abyss" (217) of Rochester's mind, so that when he asks her on the eve of their wedding whether she is afraid of "the new sphere you are about to enter?" (307), she denies it; but she does not expect to be taken, as Rochester once jestingly threatened, to the "edge of a crater" (295) in her inner landscape, and she is unprepared for what she finds there.

On her wedding morning, on the "verge" of her union with Rochester, Jane is afraid to look at herself in the mirror, but when pressed to do so she sees the image of self-estrangement: "a robed and veiled figure, so unlike my usual self that it seemed almost the image of a stranger" (315). Jane is so lost in idolatrous love of her "master" (302) that she no longer knows herself: he stands between her and the world "as an eclipse intervenes between man and the broad sun" (302). Absorbed by romanticism, Jane cannot see reality, but Bertha shocks her into recognition that she cannot surrender herself wholly to Rochester.

Bertha is both literally and metaphorically the impediment to Jane's union with Rochester. When the wedding ceremony is prevented by the declaration of an existing Mrs. Rochester, Jane is taken to see her master's other, if not better, half. She follows Rochester into previously unexplored regions of Thornfield manor where she finds the familiar "furniture" of her mind. In a room to which only Rochester, significantly, holds the key, Jane finds all the ingredients of her past self-revelations: the locked room, giant bed, well-hangings, and cabinet (320). Barely discernible, like the figures emerging from the subconscious in Jane's paintings, is a woman running backward and forward in the deepest shades at the far end of the room (321), reminding us of Jane's earlier description of herself as a "creeping creature" (251), though this one is far from deferential. As with all Jane's doubles there is a moment of identification: "I recognized well that purple face—those bloated features" (321).

Bertha Mason's extreme savagery seems gratuitous, unnecessary either to the plot (the mere existence of a wife would have prevented marriage) or to the characterization (Rochester's attempted polygamy would have been exonerated by less extreme insanity). But as Rochester struggles to control Bertha, Jane sees former fancies becoming reality: Rochester's jest that he would like to attach Jane to himself with a chain (299) is realized before her eyes as he pinions his wife to a chair with a rope, and the charade in which marriage to Rochester represented "Bridewell" (213), a famous Victorian lunatic asylum, seems to have been more than playacting. Furthermore, Jane's former "nightmare" was reality: like Adam's dream she "awoke and found it Truth." As Bertha "parted her shaggy locks from her visage" (321), Jane sees the truth and wakens from her dream.

As the young Jane recognizes the danger of succumbing to Rochester, the autobiographer presents the consequences of total surrender to her imagination without the balance of realism. Throwing herself unreservedly into the regions beyond the rational mind could result in a loss of humanity. Bertha Mason embodies the author's fear of losing control, which, ironically, would render her as ineffectual as if she were to restrict herself to surface reality. What is frightening about Bertha Mason is that she is inescapable: if the imagination is repressed it distorts and exaggerates, but overindulgence apparently has the same consequences.

Bertha's imprisonment is symbolic of the situation of the "millions" of women whom Jane declared were "condemned to a stiller doom than mine" (141), and, more important, it is a reflection of Jane's urgent need for self-expression.

Bertha's animalistic virility parodies the Victorian notion that to be truly creative is to be masculine. Jane's "genius," whether embodied in Rochester or in Bertha, is a potent force. As Phyllis Chesler says in her study of *Women and Madness*: "Madness and asylums generally function as mirror-images of the female experience, and as penalties for *being* "female" as well as desiring or daring *not* to be."[78] In Bertha, Jane sees her own desire to be unfeminine and to be engaged in active self-realization, which is why she must, until she "finds" herself again, reject Rochester. What Jane recognizes in Bertha Mason is the possible consequence of her desire to be "mastered" by an imagination stronger than her own judgment, but it is accompanied, paradoxically, by fear and resentment of this desire.

AT SEA

When Jane uncovers Bertha Mason in the deepest recesses of Thornfield manor, the autobiographer reaches the darkest regions of the self. Like Charlotte Brontë, Jane recoils in horror from what she is capable of seeing, and her reaction is similarly to stop abandoning herself to whatever she sees and to attempt to gain control: "And now I thought: till now I had only heard, seen, moved—followed up and down where I was led or dragged—watched event rush on event, disclosure open beyond disclosure: but *now, I thought*" (323). Jane had been "led," as Rochester once prophesied, to "the edge of a crater" in her visionary landscape: "I seemed to have laid me down in the dried-up bed of a great river; I heard a flood loosened in remote mountains, and I felt the torrent come" (324). The effect of her discovery of Bertha Mason is a realization of the fears depicted in her paintings: Jane is returned to the ice-bound regions of her third landscape. Nowhere else is the "scenery" of Jane's mind so manifestly incredible as when she loses Rochester:

A Christmas frost had come at midsummer; a white December storm had whirled over June; ice glazed the ripe apples, drifts crushed the blowing roses; on hayfield and cornfield lay a frozen shroud: lanes which last night blushed full of flowers, today were pathless with untrodden snow; and the woods, which twelve hours since waved leafy and fragrant as groves between the tropics, now spread, waste, wild, and white as pine-forests in wintry Norway. (323)

The world Jane had entered with Rochester was rich, fruitful, ripe, and sensuous; but it was romantic illusion. In reality her prospects are less exotic, though not as "desolate" as she now imagines.

Rochester had once prophesied that Jane would "come some day to a craggy pass in the channel, where the whole of life's stream will be broken up into whirl and tumult, foam and noise: either you will be dashed to atoms on crag points, or lifted up and borne on by some master-wave into a calmer current" (173). Jane had not appreciated the implications of her rather blasé wish to "look into the abyss, . . . explore its secrets and analyse their nature" (217); she had rather, as Rochester observed, been "Floating on with closed eyes and muffled ears, you neither see the rocks bristling not far off in the bed of the flood, nor hear the breakers boil at their base" (173), but now she fully experiences the consequences of being "self-abandoned" (324):

> The torrent poured over me. The whole consciousness of my life lorn, my love lost, my hope quenched, my faith death-struck, swayed full and mighty above me in one sullen mass. That bitter hour cannot be described: in truth, "the waters came into my soul; I sank in deep mire: I felt no standing; I came into deep waters; the floods overflowed me." (324)

The fear of drowning depicted in Jane's first landscape is not, however, realized. Although her insecurity is extreme, Jane *does* find solid ground once more, but in order to do so she must leave the "master" who has snatched it from beneath her.

ROCHESTER'S INTERRUPTED AUTOBIOGRAPHY

Jane had followed Rochester into an exotic and fabulous world. "I am to take mademoiselle to the moon," he had promised, "and there I shall seek a cave in one of the white valleys among the volcano-tops, and mademoiselle shall live with me there, and only me" (295). But the picture he had painted of their future together had been mere romanticizing—he already had a wife: "an open admission of the truth had been uttered by my master; and the living proof had been seen" (323). Now that Jane has seen the reality behind the illusion she cannot re-enter Rochester's dreamworld. Now, as he makes new plans, she listens with skepticism: "You shall go to a place I have in the south of France: a whitewashed villa on the shores of the Mediterranean. There you shall live a happy, and guarded, and most innocent life" (331).

Rochester had proposed marriage to Jane while in the middle of writing a fairy tale of their romance (295). Now that Jane knows it was nothing more than that, she cannot imagine a sequel. Rochester tries to explain his unforgivable behavior by filling in the gaps in his earlier revelations, but Jane listens with a changed heart, shocked almost to cynicism. Now when he describes his past mistresses and Bertha's degradation, Jane identifies with the women rather than with him. Jane refuses to allow Rochester to complete his story in the way he had hoped; she literally interrupts and reverses his autobiography.

The contrast between Jane's realism and Rochester's romanticism is tragically revealed in a scene in which Jane's denial of Rochester's advances is an ironic parody of the wedding ceremony:

> "Jane, do you mean to go one way in the world, and let me go another?"
>
> "I do."
>
> "Jane" (bending towards me and embracing me), "do you mean it now?"
>
> "I do."
>
> "And now?" softly kissing my forehead and cheek.
>
> "I do"—extricating myself from restraint rapidly and completely.
>
> "Oh, Jane, this is bitter! This—this is wicked. It would not be wicked to love me!"
>
> "It would to obey you." (343)

Jane's reasons for leaving Rochester are complex, but the ones she gives to pacify him are the least reliable: it is neither church nor man who arbitrates, but herself. By the time Rochester has made his desperate appeal to Jane's "magnanimity" (342) by recounting the rest of his life story, it is too late, her mind is so made up that she need not even search around for another rebuttal, she need only act on her convictions. As Rochester proceeds with the sequel to his life story he senses that Jane is not as credulous and sympathetic a listener as she has been in the past: "But, Jane, I see by your face you are not forming a very favourable opinion of me just now. You think me an unfeeling, loose-principled rake: don't you?" (338).

Rochester hopes to elicit Jane's sympathy by explaining why his wife is locked up in the attic; but his story, conveyed to the reader through Jane's newly opened eyes and underlined (or undermined) by her occasional unimpressed interjections, fails to exonerate him. The story of his relationship with Bertha is very like Jane's story of the red-room; Rochester has yet to learn the lesson in storytelling that Jane learned very early: that a "bitter and truculent" account is less convincing than a "plain" one. Telling Jane how loathsome, disgusting, boring, and degrading his past relationships have been (338) does not vindicate Rochester, but rather condemns him:

> "Hiring a mistress is the next worse thing to buying a slave: both are often by nature, and always by position, inferior: and to live familiarly with inferiors is degrading. I now hate the recollection of the time I passed with Céline, Giacinta, and Clara."
>
> I felt the truth of these words; and I drew from them the certain inference, that if I were so far as to forget myself and all the teaching that had ever been instilled into me, as—under any pretext—with any justification—through any temptation—to become the successor of these poor girls, he would one day regard me with the same feeling which now in his mind desecrated their memory. I did not give utterance to this conviction: it was enough to feel it. (339)

When Rochester reaches the part of his story where he meets "my sympathy—my better self—my good angel" (342), Jane interrupts and will not let him finish. He had forgotten the truth of what he had only just said: that though he may have "resolved to marry" Jane, her reply was "yet to be recorded in the book of Fate" (338).

Jane will not allow Rochester to anticipate the outcome of his autobiographical romance: she refuses to be his "comforter . . . rescuer" (345), to be the last mistress who would efface all past error, disprove his suspicion that "the notion of an intellectual, faithful, loving woman" was "a mere dream" (339), and thus redeem "womankind" in his eyes. What Jane will not be, finally, is Rochester's means of salvation: "Still indomitable was the reply: '*I* care for myself. The more solitary, the more friendless, the more unsustained I am, the more I will respect myself'" (344). She advises Rochester to "Do as I do: trust in God and yourself" (343), and she leaves before he can complete his story.

THE MOORS

Jane's decision to leave Rochester does not even have an attendant "solace from self-approbation"; in fact, she says, "I abhorred myself" (348). Though innocent, she feels guilty: "never may you, like me, dread to be the instrument of evil to what you wholly love" (348). The episode on the moors around Whitcross seems to be a self-inflicted punishment, the deprivation is so extreme. Not only does Jane abandon her familiar world, but she leaves her belongings on the coach and has no conception of where to go or what to do next. The episode is a paradigm of her life, described in her childhood ballad. "My feet they are sore and my limbs they are weary; Long is the way, and the mountains are wild" (54).

Jane, on "a road which led from the sun" (351), searching for food and shelter, is strikingly similar to the many representations of the "fallen woman" in Victorian paintings: wandering in a bleak landscape, expelled from human society.[79] It seems that Jane has taken upon herself the guilt of all Rochester's past mistresses and (as a sort of female Christ, or a sacrificial victim) is undergoing atonement; she refers to it as the shame of "moral degradation, blent with the physical suffering, . . . too distressing . . . to be willingly dwelt on" (355).

Perhaps, having seen Bertha Mason, Jane knows that although she is not outwardly either "unchaste" or "intemperate" (334)—Bertha's "original sins" against womanhood —she is as capable as Bertha of desiring to transgress the boundaries of what was expected of a woman. She has frequently longed immodestly for the excitements of a world beyond her domestic confines. As Charlotte Brontë herself once remarked:

> All people have their dark side—though some possess the power of throwing a fair veil over the defects; close acquaintance slowly removes the screen, and one by one the blots appear, till at length we sometimes see the pattern of perfection all slurred over with blots.[80]

Perhaps Jane refused Rochester's plea to live in his "white-washed villa" (331) in France because she knows that she herself could be like the whited "sepulchre" described in the preface as having "charnel relics" (36) within.

As the confrontation with Bertha Mason was the autobiographer's climax to the exploration of her inner selves, so the episode on the moor is the climax to the metaphorical journey beyond the "cultivated garden" of such representational art as Jane Austen's. If there are two concomitant journeys in *Jane Eyre*, that of the young protagonist and that of the mature writer, then both have reached their "limits": Jane has penetrated the darkest secret of Thornfield Manor and has discovered aspects of herself from which she recoils in horror, feelings that make it impossible to marry Rochester. The writer similarly flees from the "mastery" of romanticism back to nature, although she finds no sustenance there. The episode on the moors is also a critique of the romantic mythologizing of nature—unlike Wordsworth, who gained spiritual sustenance from the natural world, Jane confronts "Want" (351) and "death" (356). Twice before, Jane had wanted to die and had considered starving herself, but now life becomes precious: her attestation to Rochester of caring for herself is now subjected to extreme trial. It is interesting that when in her hour of temptation and extreme need Jane states, "I can but die" and "I believe in God. Let me try to wait His will in silence" (361), it is a human and not a divine voice that replies, "All men must die," thus bringing Jane back from the "other world," the "abode of people who are dead" (272), into another, very human one. Jane is about to be "reborn" into a family; her wandering directionless across wasteland is at an end.

– 8 –

MARSH END

A "PICTURE" OF DOMESTICITY

Jane has passed both literally and spiritually through the "wide bog" toward the dim light that had been shining "constant through the rain" (357) like a guiding star. At the "end" of the "marsh" Jane finds the light of reason and humanitarianism.

Even before she has met the inhabitants of Marsh End, Jane's description of her first impression of the cottage indicates a change of artistic vision. In the same way that the ideal landscapes introduced at the opening of the Thornfield chapters reveal the artistic ideals that inspire that section, Jane's vision of the interior of Marsh End, its ordinary domestic scene minutely described in loving detail, indicates her rejection of the romantic experience. As Jane approaches the house, she may well suspect an optical illusion, a kind of oasis in her desert of loneliness and starvation, offering the human support and domestic protection that she desperately seeks. Framed in the window, two young women sit "amidst the rosy peace and warmth" of the hearth (358) with their heads bent over books. How Jane must have been whisked back to the only happy times of her childhood when

Marsh End

Bessie would gather the children round the nursery fire to tell stories! "This scene was as silent as if all the figures had been shadows and the firelit apartment a picture" (358), says Jane, using an analogy that is by now familiar to the reader. Jane seems to be regarding an image of the very things she has sought throughout her life. Like Alice, she passes through the looking glass and finds that she was indeed regarding images of her own ideals: Diana and Mary are the women that Jane would like to be. At last she finds women worthy of emulation: they are neither passive like Helen Burns, nor repressed like Miss Temple, and they give Jane something she has never had before: a sense of absolute equality. They are intelligent and strong, but they do not attempt to dominate. Jane discovers the "perfect congeniality of tastes, sentiments, and principles" that she had with Rochester, but without the battle of wills:

> Indoors we agreed equally well. They were both more accomplished and better read than I was; but with eagerness I followed in the path of knowledge they had trodden before me. I devoured the books they lent me: then it was full satisfaction to discuss with them in the evening what I had perused during the day. Thought fitted thought: opinion met opinion: we coincided, in short, perfectly. (376–77)

Here is a "path of knowledge" that will not lead Jane into the "miry wilds" of her introspection. Unwilling to return to her terrifyingly lonely inner landscape, Jane clings, in this section, to the conventions of Victorian realism and avoids both the Gothicism and the charged symbolism of the previous section. If Thornfield is the most romantic section of the novel, Marsh End is its antithesis: here the autobiographer explores the possibilities of rationalism and the eighteenth century ideal that "the proper study of mankind is man." Jane's aspirations in this section are mimetic: she records, in detail, the moorland, the domestic interior, and her friends' countenances and activities. Revelations of inner lives are provided largely by external clues. Jane's gaze is directed outward; she denies as much as possible the introspective inclinations that had led to her expulsion on the moors.

The only painting Jane describes in this section is a reaction to her earlier surrealistic landscapes, a work that conforms to eighteenth-century rather than romantic ideals of art: it is a portrait of Rosamond Oliver, executed for the calculatedly didactic purpose of prompting St John to confess his love. At Marsh End Jane usually draws rather than paints: a mode peculiarly suited to "copying," and one that avoids the indulgence of imagination. Jane here treats her art as a craft rather than an inspiration: something that can be learned:

> They discovered I could draw: their pencils and color-boxes were immediately at my service. My skill, greater in this one point than theirs, surprised and charmed them. Mary would sit and watch me by the hour together: then she would take lessons: and a docile, intelligent, assiduous pupil she made. (377)

At Marsh End Jane attempts to emulate St John's self-control: like him, to make "Reason, not feeling" (401) her guide. But she finds St John (and all that he embodies) an even more exacting "master" than Rochester: if her former pain was caused by exposing too much of her inner self, her present anguish results from attempting to hide her real feelings. Jane comes to the conclusion that, contrary to St John's dictates, it could be immoral to be guided by reason and duty. Just as Jane has one more contest with a stronger character before she discovers what she values, the autobiographer has one last struggle with the attractive artistic alternative of realism, which seems, especially following the Thornfield episode, to offer greater "sanity."

As the young Jane moves into adulthood (after the rites of passage on the moor), discovering mature female companionship and rewarding intellectual pursuits, so the autobiographer moves toward greater balance by the end of the book, seeking a reconciliation of previous artistic modes. The young Jane is becoming more genuinely attentive to others. Undistorted by her fears and insecurities, her judgment of herself and others is clearer now that she is free of the romantic "web of mystification." First, however, she must recognize that the other extreme, the common-sense attitude evinced by St John Rivers, is as much a distortion of reality as Rochester's romanticism was.

St John

St John Rivers is the antithesis of Rochester: physically he embodies (in contrast to Rochester's gracelessness) classical beauty: "Greek face, very pure in outline: quite a straight, classic nose" (371); in his life St John exemplifies the Greek ideals of rationality and order. He offers Jane a model of self-control and regulation, claiming, accurately, that "Reason and not feeling, is my guide" (401).

Jane recognizes, however, that St John also has his "Bertha":

> I was sure St John Rivers—pure-lived, conscientious, zealous as he was—had not yet found that peace of God which passeth all understanding: he had no more found it, I thought, than had I, with my concealed and racking regrets for my broken idol and lost elysium—regrets to which I have latterly avoided referring, but which possessed me and tyrannized over me ruthlessly. (378–79)

Because St John has a certain sympathy with Jane, detecting in her nature "an alloy as detrimental to repose as that in mine" (381); because both are attempting to sublimate sexual desires—"Don't cling so tenaciously to ties of the flesh; save your constancy and ardor for an adequate cause" (417)—he seems to offer Jane a way to reconcile her "propensities" with her "principles" (382). When St John recommends, however, the reassuringly pragmatic task of learning Hindustani, Jane finds him an even more overbearing "master" than her last: submitting to rational pursuits is for Jane as false to her true self as surrendering wholly to imagination had been (interestingly, she compares her efforts to her art):

> I daily wished more to please him; but to do so, I felt daily more and more that I must disown half my nature, stifle half my faculties, wrest my tastes from their original bent, force myself to the

adoption of pursuits for which I had no natural vocation. . . . The thing was as impossible as to mould my irregular features to his correct and classic pattern, to give my changeable green eyes the sea-blue tint and solemn lustre of his own. (424)

Jane's new confidence in her own tastes is partly a result of her intimacy with Diana and Mary, in whom and with whom she finds a perfect balance between seriousness and pleasure: she discovers that it need not be mere self-indulgence to follow one's own inclinations. When St John criticizes Jane for looking no "higher" than "domestic endearments and household joys," she replies that these are "The best thing the world has!" (416), which is rather different from her sentiments at Thornfield when she longed to escape the domestic sphere.

St John confirms for Jane what she had suspected even as a child: that denying the flesh does not necessarily elevate the soul. He constantly exhorts her to look beyond this world with its "ties of the flesh": "St John was a good man; but I began to feel he had spoken truth of himself when he said he was hard and cold. The humanities and amenities of life had no attraction for him—its peaceful enjoyments no charm" (418). Jane recognizes that St John's commitment to his duty, his grim refusal to take pleasure in ordinary things, "damped me" (418): "As I looked at his lofty forehead, still and pale as a white stone—at his fine lineaments fixed in study—I comprehended all at once that he would hardly make a good husband" (418). Jane concludes that beneath his masquelike face St John is indeed "inexorable as death" (383).

THE PORTRAIT OF ROSAMOND OLIVER

With great clarity, Jane recognizes at Marsh End certain things about herself:

I never in my life have known any medium in my dealings with positive, hard characters, antagonistic to my own, between absolute

submission and determined revolt. I have always faithfully observed
the one, up to the very moment of bursting, sometimes with vol-
canic vehemence into the other. (426)

One cannot avoid thinking, in this penetrating self-analysis, of Bertha
Mason's eruption into the autobiography. Jane does not, however, so
clearly recognize that St John, in his struggle to suffocate love for
Rosamond Oliver, is offering her another of the many parodies of her
own life's events, enacting for her an extreme version of her resistance
to, and rejection of, Rochester. Accustomed to seeing what lies beneath the surface, Jane quickly becomes aware that St John is in love
with Rosamond, and, perhaps remembering how she had realized her
love for Rochester by gazing at his portrait, she intends to do the same
for St John by presenting him with Rosamond's likeness and then advising him to "take to yourself the original at once" (398). But Jane is
unprepared for St John's stoicism and fixity of purpose as strong as
her own. Rosamond would not make a good missionary's wife, and
St John affirms the eighteenth-century ideal that "Natural affection
only, of all the sentiments, has permanent power over me" (401).

Jane later gazes in "wonder" as St John describes how the "battle" against his desire for Rosamond had been "won"; yet she too
could have used the same words to describe leaving Rochester:

> I rested my temples on the breast of temptation and put my neck
> voluntarily under her yoke of flowers; I tasted her cup. The pillow
> was burning: there is an asp in the garland: the wine has a bitter
> taste: her promises are hollow—her offers false: I see and know all
> this. (399)

A New Life Story Narrated

While Jane is teaching the Morton Village School under the
pseudonym of Miss Elliott, St John visits her with a story of which he
is impatient "to hear the sequel"; he comes to complete and transform
Jane's autobiography:

On reflection, I find the matter will be better managed by my assuming the narrator's part, and converting you into a listener. Before commencing, it is but fair to warn you that the story will sound somewhat hackneyed in your ears; but stale details often regain a degree of freshness when they pass through new lips. For the rest, whether trite or novel, it is short. (405)

Jane listens incredulously to the story of an anonymous orphan left in the lap of "charity" who inherits a fortune. "Really it strikes me there are parallel points in her history and yours" (406), observes St John in the only humorous comment he ever makes. The matter-of-fact style in which he delivers Jane's history makes it seem even stranger to her ears, and she is shocked as the account of a grimly realistic struggle turns into a fairy tale. Jane, it seems, has a fairy godfather; she is now being sought by the solicitor Mr. Briggs:

> "Merely to tell you that your uncle, Mr Eyre of Madeira, is dead; that he has left you all his property, and that you are now rich— merely that—nothing more."
> "I!—rich?"
> "Yes, you rich—quite an heiress." (407)

Jane is astonished; not only by the inheritance, but by the fact that the Rivers, to whom she feels more akin even than to Rochester, are indeed her family. Jane need no longer be "a wanderer on the face of the earth" (256). She has a home (which she immediately sets about restoring), and a family.

Thus, in a matter of minutes, Jane's life story is altered for her; her autobiography must be revised, and she must acknowledge that the portrait she has presented of herself as "disconnected, poor and plain" has been founded on a lie. She is, in fact, none of these things: she has family, fortune, and an eligible admirer. The person responsible for closing up the gap between the appearance and the reality of Jane's life is her Uncle John.

John Eyre of Madeira

"Destiny stands by sarcastic, with our dramatis personae folded in her hands," says George Eliot in *Middlemarch*,[81] and no doubt Jane feels a similar sense of irony to discover that there has been all along another uncle who could determine her destiny as much as Uncle Reed had. John Eyre is probably the most important "dramatis personae" in Jane's life, and, although he never actually appears, he more than any other character influences the plot of *Jane Eyre*. If Charlotte Brontë is to be identified with any character in the novel, it is not Jane (as is customarily assumed), but the uncle who has lurked behind the scenes, exerting a decisive influence on events, unknown to Jane, at every crucial turn.

If we look back over Jane's past, we will see that her Uncle John had, like Bertha Mason, been continually attempting to make contact with Jane and to make himself known to her; but even though she had been told of his existence, Jane did not (as Rochester once observed) avail herself of her possible good fortune, probably because she was as oblivious to it as she was to the malevolence embodied in Bertha Mason.

Jane's Aunt Reed had confessed, on her deathbed, that three years previously (while Jane was at Lowood School) she had received a letter from John Eyre requesting

> the address of my niece. . . . It is my intention to write shortly and desire her to come to me at Madeira. Providence has blessed my endeavours to secure a competency: and as I am unmarried and childless, I wish to adopt her during my life, and bequeath her at my death whatever I may have to leave. (266–67)

Although the letter impressed Jane enough for her to later quote it in full in the autobiography, she did not attempt to contact her uncle to contradict her aunt's lie that she had died of typhus at the school (although she did, during her engagement to Rochester, think of writing to her uncle to discover whether she could perhaps become financially dent). The same Mr. Briggs who had intercepted Jane's marriage must have informed John Eyre that she was alive.

If Bertha is the projection of Jane's fears, Uncle John is the realization of her wildest hopes: not until after Bertha has revealed herself, and Jane confronts those emotions she has suppressed, are Uncle John's benefits bestowed on her, so that finally there is a correspondence between her inner liberation from oppressive self-restraint and her outward, external, liberation and independence.

All along it has been Uncle John who has held the "key" to the truth about Jane Eyre: that she indeed already possessed, unknown to herself, the things she was in search of: family, friends, and financial independence; but Jane, unable to see herself as anything other than "disconnected, poor, plain," was, until now, ill-prepared for the truth. Thus, John Eyre is the crux of the plot—the central, yet obscured, hinge to the events in Jane's life.

ANOTHER INTERRUPTED AUTOBIOGRAPHY

Throughout the autobiography Jane has been presented from various perspectives: through the eyes of others as well as her own mature ones. This has not only provided a complex "portrait" of the artist-heroine but has also continually drawn attention to the possible distortions of the truth. The reader thereby derives a sense of the difference between the superficial appearance of a person's life and its underlying reality. Mrs. Reed saw Jane as a "sickly, whining, pining thing" (260), whereas Rochester regarded her as "a keen . . . daring" and "independent" woman (340). Jane, fearing the inaccuracy of both accounts, has rejected the onus of being idealized as much as she rejected the burden of being despised. Now, she is offered another account of herself that doesn't "ring true."

Once again Jane and the man she is connected with have privately conjectured the sequel to their personal history, and once again the stories do not coincide. St John has determined that Jane shall be his wife and go with him to India, not because he loves her, but because she has the necessary qualities: "I watch your career with interest, because I consider you a specimen of a diligent, orderly, energetic woman" (401). St John prefaces his marriage proposal with an account very similar to Rochester's story of how he has covertly observed Jane's behavior: "I recognized a soul that revelled in the flame and excitement of sacrifice. . . . Jane you are docile, diligent, disinterested, faithful, constant, and courageous; very gentle, and very heroic" (429). Jane does not recognize herself in this flattering but distorted picture: St John, according to his own bias, has denied the spontaneous (and even selfish) pleasure that Jane derives from her actions.

When St John explains that his interest in Jane is not "because I deeply compassionate what you have gone through," but because "I honour endurance, perseverance, industry, talent," she intimates that his stoicism is a Greek rather than a Christian ideal—"You would describe yourself as a mere pagan philosopher" (401)—knowing that this would disconcert him.

When St John insists she should be his wife, Jane sees clearly what she had only intuitively sensed about Rochester: "He prizes me as a soldier would a good weapon" (430). Jane retorts with what in retrospect she considers "repressed sarcasm": "Oh! I will give my heart to God. . . . You do not want it" (431). As Jane listens to St John's well-rehearsed rhetoric the "veil" of her illusions is torn down almost as violently as it was with Rochester:

> Revelations were being made in this conference: the analysis of his nature was proceeding before my eyes. I saw his fallibilities: I comprehended them. . . . The veil fell from his hardness and despotism. Having felt in him the presence of these qualities, I felt his imperfection, and took courage. (432)

Once again Jane interrupts the narrator in the midst of his autobiographical revelation, and once again she disappoints him of the intended outcome. St John is as obstinate as Rochester in his desire to marry Jane, although instead of attempting to manipulate her heart, he employs repeated rhetorical attacks, believing that Jane's "honour," her moral conscience, will be as vulnerable as his own: "you may still be spared the dishonor of breaking your promise" (439). But Jane remains clear-headed: "Now I never had, as the reader knows, either given any formal promise or entered into any engagement; and this language was all much too hard and much too despotic for the occasion" (439). Jane can only counter St John's obstinacy with an extreme protest: she "finished the business" (438) by telling him "you almost hate me. If I were to marry you, you would kill me. You are killing me now" (438). St John is shocked by Jane's vehement emotion: "Your words are such as ought not to be used: violent, unfeminine, and untrue. They betray an unfortunate state of mind: they merit severe reproof" (438). But even in the midst of his disappointed hopes St John is true to his principle of rationality and "controlled his passion perfectly" (439).

The autobiographer recalls that she had been "thrust" by St John "at once to the point I had so long shunned. I was tempted to cease struggling with him—to rush down the torrent of his will into the gulf of his existence, and there lose my own" (443). Jane sees that the temptation to surrender her identity to St John's is almost as strong as it had been with Rochester: "I was a fool both times. To have yielded then would have been an error of principle; to have yielded now would have been an error of judgement" (443). In yielding to Rochester Jane would have betrayed her principles, yielding to St John would betray her judgment: the distinction is interesting, since these were the very aspects on which each man argued his case. Rochester, the romantic, appealed to Jane's inner sense of right—her private moral feelings; whereas St John, the pragmatist, appeals to her reason.

In retrospect the autobiographer acknowledges that her attraction to St John resulted from her own aspirations toward self-denial and self-control; that just as Rochester had come along in answer to her intense desire for excitement, St John satisfied her reaction, her need to control her emotions. Although Jane feels that she was "right when I adhered to principle and law, and scorned and crushed the insane promptings of a frenzied moment" (386), she has been pushed too far in the other direction. In submitting to St John, Jane had striven to cleave only to reason. Charlotte Brontë herself had once "determined to take Nature and Truth as my sole guides. . . . I restrained imagination, eschewed romance, repressed excitement" but she discovered that her imagination would not be silenced: it was "a strong restless faculty which claims to be heard" (L, 329–30). Jane has similarly been restraining her imagination and struggling to deny her love for Rochester; but just as she is about to "take Nature and Truth" as her sole guides, to submit to St John's rational utilitarian principles, she hears the voice of her imagination calling so strongly that it cannot be resisted or denied. The voice is so urgent and distinct that she runs out into the garden, and, significantly for the metaphorical journey, "the hills beyond March Glen sent the answer faintly back" (445). Minutes previously Jane had been inwardly lost, contending with "my inward dimness of vision, before which clouds yet rolled. . . . 'Show me, show me the path!' I entreated of Heaven" (444); but the gloom of her inner landscape is lifted, and she sees that "the path" leads back to Rochester.

The author recalls this as an awakening: "it acted on my senses as if their utmost activity hitherto had been but torpor, from which they were now summoned and forced to wake" (444). Because she has denied her imaginative faculty, Jane has been only half alive. The call is an affirmation of her intuition, a celebration of what Brontë called "the unseen seat of life"; it represents the novel's imminent return to romanticism.

– 9 –

FERNDEAN:
RETRACING THE PATH

THE RUINED HOUSE

Jane believes that the cry she had heard was neither "superstition" nor "a miracle," but "nature . . . doing her best" (445). She explains it to herself as an inner faculty, clearly that of imagination, which had released her imprisoned soul:

> It seemed in *me*—not in the external world. I asked was it a mere nervous impression—a delusion? I could not conceive or believe: it was more like an inspiration. The wondrous shock of feeling had come like the earthquake which shook the foundations of Paul and Silas's prison; it had opened the doors of the soul's cell and loosed its bands—it had wakened it out of its sleep. (446)

Rochester had similarly likened Jane's soul to a captive creature in a "clay dwelling place":

> I cannot get at it—the savage beautiful creature! If I tear, if I rend the slight prison, my outrage will only let the captive loose. Conqueror I might be of the house; but the inmate would escape to

heaven before I could call myself possessor of its clay dwelling-place. (344–45)

Jane's soul, liberated from the restraints she has vainly imposed on it at Marsh End, leads her "like the messenger pigeon" (447) back "home." Both literally and metaphorically Jane retraces her path: she retrieves her former romanticism and revives her belief in "the sympathies of Nature with man" (249). "Who would be hurt by my once more tasting the life his glance can give me?" (448–49), says Jane, to rationalize acting on her "inspiration." As she awaits the coach to Thornfield, she hears it "approach from a great distance" just as she had once heard Rochester "amidst the silence of those solitary roads and desert hills" (447). She observes: "It was the same vehicle whence, a year ago, I had alighted one summer evening on this very spot, how desolate, and hopeless, and objectless!" (447). Just as she had traveled from Thornfield to Gateshead, Jane feels once more that she must go back in order to go forward. She approaches Thornfield in the same manner she had the last time she returned, unannounced, mentally anticipating each familiar landmark on the way (272; 449), hoping to steal unseen upon the house.

What Jane sees is expressed in an analogy so carefully detailed, and so emphatically introduced, that she is clearly anxious to impress it on the reader's mind:

> Hear an illustration, reader.
> A lover finds his mistress asleep on a mossy bank; he wishes to catch a glimpse of her fair face without waking her. He steals softly over the grass, careful to make no sound; he pauses—fancying she has stirred: he withdraws: not for worlds would he be seen. All is still: he again advances: he bends above her; a light veil rests on her features: he lifts it, bends lower; now his eyes anticipate the vision of beauty—warm and blooming, and lovely, in rest. How hurried was their first glance! But how they fix! How he starts! How he suddenly and vehemently clasps in both arms the form he dared not, a moment since, touch with his finger! How he calls aloud a name, and drops his burden, and gazes on it wildly! He thus grasps, and cries, and gazes, because he no longer fears to waken by any sound

he can utter—by any movement he can make. He thought his love slept sweetly: he finds she is stone dead. (449)

If this is merely for Gothic atmosphere it is inordinately long. It is clearly the climax to the metaphoric implications of the house and the veil that have been used throughout the novel. Jane had returned to Thornfield to search not only for someone she loved, but for something else that seemed to be a part of herself: the self that she had left behind when she fled Thornfield. But what she finds when she lifts the veil is "a blackened ruin": it seems that Jane's "house," the house of her soul, has been purged by fire: "The front was, as I had once seen it in a dream, but a shell-like wall, very high and fragile-looking . . . all had crashed-in" (449–50). Wanting to know "what loss, besides mortar and marble and woodwork had followed upon it" (450), Jane seeks information from the local innkeeper and once again has the strange sensation of hearing her "own story" from an external source (451). Jane learns, as she should have guessed, that Bertha Mason had caused the fire:

> She set fire first to the hangings of the room next her own, and then she got down to a lower story, and made her way to the chamber that had been the governess's—(she was like as if she knew somehow how matters had gone on, and had a spite at her). (452)

The innkeeper uncannily blames Jane, both as the ultimate source of Mrs. Rochester's resentment and as the cause of Mr. Rochester's present suffering: "I have often wished that Miss Eyre had been sunk in the sea before she came to Thornfield Hall" (453), he concludes, little knowing that he is speaking to the culprit and that she had in fact sunk in her own sea. Bertha, the embodiment of an uncontrolled imagination, has burnt herself out: Jane learns that she is "dead as the stones on which her brains and blood were scattered" (453). If Rochester is the "rock" of Jane's mind, Bertha "Mason" is the "stone," or imagination without love.

RECONCILIATION

Thus the source of violence in the novel had finally turned in on itself and destroyed itself, facilitating a return to the equilibrium with which we associate "comic" resolutions. But Rochester had been maimed by the fire of Jane' anger as he had been tormented by her cruel rejection. Rochester as well as Jane had been only half-alive during the absence: "He walked just like a ghost about the grounds and in the orchard, as if he had lost his senses" (452). As the embodiment of romanticism, Rochester had been seriously distorted by the frenzy of Bertha Mason.

Throughout the account of Jane's reconciliation with Rochester, there is emphasis on their completion of one another. Jane says she has come to "rehumanize" Rochester, but she also is "whole" for the first time: "she is all here: her heart too" (458), she affirms. "You touch me sir:—you hold me and fast enough: I am not cold like a corpse nor vacant like air, am I?" (459). This is not Jane "air" but Jane the "heir," the first truly substantial portrait: "I am independent, sir, as well as rich: I am my own mistress." At last Jane has achieved her integrity, a substantial sense of her independent status, emotionally as well as practically. She is, however, only truly herself with Rochester; only now can she begin to express her whole nature:

> There was no harassing restraint, no repressing of glee and vivacity with him; for with him I was at perfect ease, because I knew I suited him; all I said or did seemed either to console or revive him. Delightful consciousness! It brought to life and light my whole nature: in his presence I thoroughly lived; and he lived in mine. (461)

Thus begins the most important phase of Jane's artistic development and the most decisive move toward becoming a writer. Because Rochester cannot see, Jane begins the lasting habit of translating her visual perceptions into words: "He saw nature—he saw books through me; and never did I weary of gazing for his behalf, and of putting into words the effect of field, tree, town, river, cloud, sunbeam—of the landscape before us" (476). Jane can no longer paint pictures for Rochester: instead she must learn "word-painting"; this necessity inaugurates the tendency already developed by her imagination toward an increasingly narrative mode.

Returning to Rochester effects a transformation of Jane's mental landscape: the bleak and desolate rocks of her youth, and even the empty moors surrounding her, are replaced by open fields: "I led him out of the wet and wild wood into some cheerful fields: I described to him how brilliantly green they were; how the flowers and hedges looked refreshed; how sparklingly blue was the sky" (464). This surely is "Paradise Regained"; Jane's inner journey has terminated: she has passed from a confined and frozen interior out into the most frightening of remote regions and has arrived finally in a benign, expansive landscape.

The conclusion to *Jane Eyre* must not be underestimated: we have examined the pattern of symbolism by which the young Jane's search for herself is concurrently the mature autobiographer's search for an artistic identity. Jane's authenticity is achieved with Rochester only when she is reconciled to the strong desire to be with him. By returning to Rochester Jane validates "the deeper shade of the supernatural" that caused their reunion. The inexplicable voice that had called to Jane was surely the voice of her own imagination, that same voice that Brontë described to Lewes in defense of the Gothic aspects in *Jane Eyre*:

> Sir, is not the real experience of each individual very limited? . . . Then, too, imagination is a strong, restless faculty, which claims to be heard and exercised: are we to be quite deaf to her cry, and insensate to her struggles? When she shows us bright pictures, are we never to look at them, and try to reproduce them? And when she is eloquent, and speaks rapidly and urgently in our ear, are we not to write to her dictation? (L, 330)

Brontë's new confidence in her artistic ideals is here so strong that she uses rhetorical questions; there could be no clearer confirmation of her romantic conception of the artist writing under the pressure of inspiration. Once Jane, at the end of the novel, is reconciled to those romantic yearnings she had attempted to deny, she "finds" her true self both personally and artistically:

> I know what it is to live entirely for and with what I love best on earth. I hold myself supremely blest—blest beyond what language can express; because I am my husband's life as fully as he is mine. . . . We talk, I believe, all day long: to talk to each other is but a more animated and an audible thinking. (475–76)

Rochester is almost a part of Jane's self, "perfect concord is the result" (476), both externally and internally. Jane is at last fully integrated: the dual perspective ends when the autobiographer tells us, "I have now been married ten years" (475).

At last Jane can commence "the narrative of my experiences" (464), knowing that she alone will finish it, that it will not be appropriated by those who wish to shape it to their own ends, as Rochester and St John had attempted. Jane assures Rochester that "to leave my tale half-told, will, you know, be a sort of security that I shall appear at your breakfast-table to finish it" (463). The rather extravagant declarations of a fairy-tale conclusion to the romance between Jane and Rochester must also be seen as Jane's mature recognition of all aspects of herself: as Rochester is made "whole" (his sight is restored and he becomes less crippled) physically, Jane is made whole emotionally, each in the presence of the other. Recalling the insubstantial self in the red-room Jane asks, "I am not cold like a corpse, nor vacant like air, am I?" (459).

Nothing could more emphatically affirm that Jane had been right to follow the voice of inspiration within her rather than the urgings of St John's reason from without. Although attending to her "master" "was to indulge my sweetest wishes" (476), it also, it seems, was capable of restoring sight to the blind. Meanwhile, St John's decision to follow his "Master" (477) was having less success. In what would otherwise be a strangely superfluous ending to the novel, Jane cannot resist a last "I told you so" to St John, whose parting words to Jane—that though her spirit was willing her flesh was weak (446)—had summarized their differences. St John's flesh, it seems, is equally weak; there is unmistakable irony in Jane's eulogy of the "resolute, indefatigable, pioneer" (477) who is dying. As Jane sits down to write her autobiography, attempting to come to terms with what Harold Bloom has called "the anxiety of influence,"[82] St John, the embodiment of reason, withers beneath the Indian sun. While St John's "Master" is calling him to his death, Jane is giving new life to hers.

THE ENDING

Jane concludes then, not with the "Happily ever after" ending that we expect from romance, but with a postscript in which she imagines, not without a great deal of irony, St John dying. The otherwise inexplicable and awkward conclusion suggests that Brontë is interested in the symbolic as well as the realistic aspects of her characters, and in the way in which they help to define Jane's artistic conclusions.

The final pages close the gap between Jane and the autobiographer and bring the reader right into the writing time: "My tale draws to its close: one word respecting my experience of married life, and one brief glance at the fortunes of those whose names have most frequently recurred in this narrative, and I have done" (475). Jane will not "have done" until she concludes the struggle with the two "masters" who have represented her internal conflict. The contrast between her relationships with Rochester and St John in the closing paragraphs indicates Jane's mature artistic ideals. The strongest indictment of St John's principles resides in Jane's reaction to the last letter she ever received from him, which "drew from my eyes human tears and yet filled my heart with divine joy" (477). Her response, unlike St John's rational affection and cool self-control, is spontaneous and emotional, a response of the human animal, and yet it inspires in her a religious feeling. Unlike St John, Jane clearly believes that the soul can be aroused through the flesh. Because of her near-idolatrous relationship with her husband—"I know what it is to live entirely for and with what I love best on earth" (475)—Jane considers herself "supremely blest" (475). The belief that the body and the soul are inextricably related has inspired the whole autobiography. Indeed, Jane could not have embarked on a simultaneously inner and outer exploration without the conviction that the one implied the other.

Jane's journey in search of herself ends, then, with Rochester in open fields: "the landscape before us," which as always indicates Jane's prospects, is unspecified "field, tree, town, river, cloud, sunbeam" (476), creating a feeling of unprecedented liberty. Gone are the intimidating blue mountain peaks, white preternaturally long roads, and boggy moors that Jane once could not see her way through; and gone also are the storms and rough seas that characterized her inner explorations.

With St John, Jane had said her mind felt like a "rayless dungeon, with one shrinking fear fettered in its depths" (428); her fear that his rigidity would eventually "kill" was apparently justified. St John is still the "indefatigable pioneer . . . amidst rocks and dangers" (477), but his world is all sun and heat, and nothing can live. "Like a giant," he "hews down the prejudices" of others; but his work is all destructive, and ultimately self-destructive—"his glorious sun hastens to its setting" (477). Rochester, on the other hand, is being born anew: "the sky is no longer a blank to him—the earth no longer a void" (476). The images of light and sight suggest differences in the men's "vision": Rochester was blinded by introspection, but St John died because he refused to look inward.

– 10 –

SOME CONCLUSIONS

Why did Elizabeth Rigby, on her contemporaries' behalf, disclaim the "tone" of *Jane Eyre* as one that had "overthrown authority and violated every code human and divine" (CH, 109–10)? What was it that outraged Brontë's readers if, as one critic contended, the obvious "moral" of the novel is that "laws, both human and divine, approved in our calmer moments, are not to be disobeyed when our time of trial comes" (CH, 79). Does Jane, finally, conform to, or challenge, existing moral law?

The answer is that, in carrying out the purpose avowed in the preface of "plucking . . . the mask from the face of the Pharisee" (35), of exposing hypocrisy, especially of a religious kind, the novel implicitly challenges all aspects of the status quo subsumed under the Christian tradition, thereby revealing the arbitrariness of the Victorians' most cherished beliefs and institutions (defended more fiercely in the face of Darwin's discoveries). Although *Jane Eyre* is peppered with professions of orthodox faith, it was possible for Elizabeth Rigby to maintain that it was "anti-Christian" and "rebellious": we must clearly examine the evidence in the text very closely.

Jane's beliefs are put under extreme pressure during the two major moral crises in the novel—the two decisions to leave the men who want to marry her. The intensity of these crises is created by the condensed allusions to other problems previously confronted by Jane in the novel, predominantly the question of what she could reasonably (or unreasonably) expect of her life as a woman and the very conflicting (horrified yet sympathetic) attitude that she had toward Bertha Mason's madness. In the two key passages in which Jane leaves first Rochester and then St John, links are established between masculine identity, which advocates a repressive moral "Law" based on reason, and feminine identity, which is flexible, intuitive, and able to embrace paradox.

Although when Jane leaves Rochester she claims it is because of "law," because of the divine and secular injunction against polygamy, she rescinds this by later returning to him not knowing that circumstances have changed. It is clear that what Jane offered as an explanation to Rochester at the time—especially in view of his intense agitation (344)—is not to be trusted. The statement "I will keep the law given by God; sanctioned by man" (344) is just that—the voice of "conscience and reason turned traitors against me" (344), a received yet internalized morality that speaks contrary to Jane's desires. Whenever Jane is most acutely insecure, close to despair, she doubts her own intuition: in the red-room, for example, she wondered whether she was wicked since "all said I was" (48). At such times Jane grasps at orthodox expressions of faith. Nothing could be less convincing, more embarrassing, than Jane's formal and self-conscious utterance on the Rivers' doorstep, "I can but die, . . . and I believe in God. Let me try to wait His will in silence" (361), especially since it is spoken aloud. Until this moment Jane had been outcast from all protective influence, bereft of her heavenly Father, and the phrase signifies her stepping back into the safety of a secular family.

The decision to leave Rochester is repeated and reversed by the decision to leave St John. Both leave-takings exhibit the same pattern: each time the man recounts his past and tells Jane that he has observed her voyeuristically and that she possesses the qualities that would complement himself. Both times Jane interrupts and seizes power over her lover, angering him with her intractability, asserting her right to determine her own life. Thus Jane undermines the Victorian ideal, inherited from the Christian tradition, that the woman (being irrational) should be guided by the man; she furthermore asserts the validity of her emotions, and even passions, above common sense, and it is this that aligns her with Bertha Mason's "madness." The second decision to leave St John and return to her former lover reveals that Jane is, and perhaps always has been, willing to transgress moral "law" in order to fulfill her own needs, although the first time they happened to correspond to social dictates.

What Jane rejects in both Rochester and St John is their inability to see her as she really is; they can only see her as a necessary complement, an accessory, to themselves. Whereas the men fail to recognize their subjectivity, Jane has continually drawn attention to hers throughout the novel. The men, furthermore, are so sure of the rightness of their own views and needs that they are both outraged when Jane will not conform (although Rochester is denied St John's righteous indignation).

Because for Jane each man embodies an aspect of herself (she recognizes as they do not the tendency to project our own fears and aspirations onto others), deciding to leave is experienced as alienation from herself, as inner division (until the break is actually made). The pain she feels is a kind of schizophrenia in which her inner voices "clamored wildly" (344) and "Conscience, turned tyrant, held Passion by the throat . . . and swore that with that arm of iron he would thrust her down to unsounded depths of agony" (325) (notice that Conscience is masculine and Passion is feminine). When Jane is extricating herself from Rochester's "hand of fiery iron" (342), she is literally beside herself, decentered, and feels that she is mad. "I am insane . . . quite insane" (344); "only an idiot" would succumb (345). Needing fervently to retrieve her reason, Jane grasps at the normalcy of a widely approved tradition:

> I will hold to the principles received by me when I was sane, and
> not mad—as I am now. Laws and principles are not for times when

> there is no temptation: they are for such moments as this, when
> body and soul rise in mutiny against their rigour; stringent are they;
> inviolate they shall be. If at my individual convenience I might
> break them, what would be their worth? . . . Preconceived opinions,
> foregone determinations are all I have at this hour to stand by; there
> I plant my foot. (344)

Feeling intensely insecure, she wishes only to be led, to step back inside
the safe confines of acceptable behavior, and embrace the patriarchal
code handed down from God to man.

It is not until the second episode of rejection that it becomes clear
Jane had been clutching at straws. St John is the embodiment of, and
finally functions to parody, the "law given by God, sanctioned by
man" (344). Indeed he wishes to perpetrate even finer distinctions in
the hierarchy by handing his beliefs down to Jane, to woman. St John
believes absolutely in the will of God, in Truth that has a single author,
and is therefore incontrovertible. He offers Jane the attractive possibility of feeling unified and single-minded as opposed to divided and
conflicted: "My work, which had appeared so vague, so hopelessly
diffuse, condensed itself as he proceeded, and assumed a definite form
under his shaping hand" (429). But in an allusion to the former "iron
grip" of moral law (the masculine principle of Jane's inner conflict;
Passion is a "she"), Jane recognizes the repression that would be a kind
of living death: "My iron shroud contracted round me" (429). When
St John claims Jane "not for my pleasure, but for my Sovereign's service" (428), he is offering her the opportunity of fulfilling her previous
declaration to Rochester that she would keep the "law given by God,
sanctioned by man," but Jane sees that it would be a self-sacrifice
amounting to death: "if I *do* make the sacrifice he urges, I will make
it absolutely: I will throw all on the altar—heart, vitals, the entire
victim" (430). When Jane tells St John that if she were to marry him
he would "kill" her—"You are killing me now" (438)—he accuses her
of being so "unfeminine" as to be verging on insanity: "*I should kill
you—I am killing you?* Your words are such as ought not to be used:
violent, unfeminine, and untrue. They betray an unfortunate state of
mind: they merit severe reproof" (438). When Jane tells St John that

she will return to Rochester, a man who, as Elizabeth Rigby said, "deliberately and secretly seeks to violate the laws of both God and man," he says he will pray that she "may not indeed become a castaway" (439–40).

Earlier Jane had asked what "worth" there would be to laws that could be broken "at my individual convenience"; a question she answers by returning to Rochester. We have seen that adherence to the moral law, to reason, to the "iron shroud" of patriarchal tradition, is so repressive as to be for Jane equivalent to "suicide": "such a martyrdom would be monstrous" (430). She refuses to submit to the wills of God or the men in her life: "It was *my* time to assume ascendancy. *My* powers were in play and in force" (445). Powers that were to culminate in the fictional autobiography.

THE PREFACE TO THE SECOND EDITION

The preface that Charlotte Brontë wrote to the second edition of *Jane Eyre*, in response to the criticism evoked by the work, can only be appreciated retrospectively. Having read the novel, we recognize that the preface is a microcosm and indeed a parody of the work as a whole, one that furthermore establishes an analogy between the fictional authoress and her autobiographical work. The preface indicates the source of the tension in the novel between what is stated literally and the contradictory emotional reaction it arouses in its readers: it is a contradiction between what is said and what is achieved. Everything that is stated in the opening of the preface is retracted by the end, exposing not only Jane's mask of candor but also the novel's own pretensions to "plainness." Thus we are warned by the preface to be on our guard against Jane's, and the novel's, disingenuousness or naïveté. The preface, though signed by its male "editor" Currer Bell, nevertheless reveals a persona remarkably like Jane's: diffident, modest, and yet rigidly moralistic in its judgment of others. Not only does the fictional personality that is created echo Jane's, but so too does its writing style, even to the extent that it employs the now famous and distinctive direct address to the "Reader."

Some Conclusions

The preface opens on a diffident note, thanking the "Public, for the indulgent ear it has inclined to a plain tale with few pretensions," the "Press, for the fair field its honest suffrage has opened to an obscure aspirant," and finally "my Publishers" (whose?) "for the aid and . . . liberality afforded to an unknown and unrecommended Author" (35). Only the last statement has any truth in it: by this time the "obscure" aspirant had achieved notoriety for her outrageous and anything but "plain tale." The "editor," however (and we are by this time not distinguishing), attributes to the authoress those very qualities that Jane (falsely) arrogates to herself throughout the novel: humility, obscurity, plainness (these are also the characteristics of the novel). The plain and unknown tale is the inevitable product of a similarly powerless, insignificant, artist-heroine.

It is soon clear, however, that the same hidden "passion" that informs the novel erupts into the preface as intense moral indignation against those who have misunderstood and maltreated the novel in much the same manner as Jane herself had been misunderstood and maltreated. Once the "passion" is released, it turns everything on its head: the humility becomes arrogance, and the gratitude resentment. The "editor" turns on "the timorous or carping few who doubt the tendency" of *Jane Eyre* and claims nothing less than the fame and function of a prophet, who we know is always hated in his own land: "The world may not like to see . . . ideas dissevered. . . . It may hate him who dares to scrutinise and expose . . . but hate as it will, it is indebted to him" (35–36). Thus the "obscure aspirant" claims universal notoriety. Similarly a "plain tale with few pretensions," as it had been described at the opening of the preface, could hardly hope to achieve the later-stated purpose of definitively separating and outlining good and evil, truth and appearance.

Thus the preface states that the mission of the novel is no modest one: "To pluck the mask from the face of the Pharisee" and "to penetrate the sepulchre and reveal charnel relics" beneath. Appropriately, the preface plucks away its own humble mask to expose its self-confident ambition.

NOTES AND REFERENCES

1. Quoted in Miriam Allott, ed., *The Brontës: The Critical Heritage* (London and Boston: Routledge & Kegan Paul, 1974), 89. For ease of reference all subsequent quotations from this work are cited in the text using the abbreviation CH.

2. For background see Brian Inglis, *Poverty and the Industrial Revolution* (London: Hodder & Stoughton, 1981).

3. Charlotte Brontë, *Jane Eyre*, ed. Q. D. Leavis (1847; reprint, Harmondsworth: Penguin Books, 1985), 116. All subsequent references to *Jane Eyre* are cited in the text from this edition.

4. M. Jeanne Peterson, "The Victorian Governess: Status Incongruence in Family and Society," in *Suffer and Be Still: Women in the Victorian Age,* ed. Martha Vicinus (Bloomington and London: Indiana Press, 1973), 3–19.

5. Clement Shorter, ed., *The Brontës Life and Letters*, 2 vols. (London: Hodder & Stoughton, 1908), 1:159.

6. Peterson, "Victorian Governess," 13, n.48.

7. Walter E. Houghton, *The Victorian Frame of Mind, 1830–1870* (New Haven and New London: Yale University Press, 1957), 191.

8. Elizabeth Gaskell, *The Life of Charlotte Brontë*, ed. Alan Shelston (1924; reprint, Harmondsworth: Penguin Books, 1975), 458. For ease of reference all subsequent quotations from this work are cited in the text using the abbreviation L.

9. Margot Peters, *Unquiet Soul: A Biography of Charlotte Brontë* (New York: Doubleday & Co., 1975), 60.

10. See Gaskell, *Life*, 308, where Brontë tells her sisters she would create a heroine different from all expectations.

11. Frederic Kenyon, ed., *Letters of Elizabeth Barrett Browning*, 2 vols. (London: Smith Elder & Co., 1897), 1:232.

12. Thomas Wise and John Symington, eds., *The Brontës: Their Lives, Friendships and Correspondences*, 4 vols. (1932; reprint, 4 vols in 2, Oxford: Basil Blackwell, Shakespeare Head Press, 1980), 2:255.

13. *Coleridge: Poetical Works*, ed. Ernest Hartley Coleridge (London, Oxford, New York: Oxford University Press, 1969), 65.

14. David Carroll, ed., *George Eliot: The Critical Heritage* (London: Routledge & Kegan Paul, 1971), 162.

15. Amy Cruse, *The Victorians and Their Reading* (1930; reprint, Boston and Cambridge: Riverside Press, 1963), 263.

16. Robert Heilman, "Charlotte Brontë's 'New' Gothic," in *From Jane Austen to Joseph Conrad*, ed. Robert C. Rathburn and Martin Steinmann, Jr. (Minneapolis: University of Minnesota Press, 1958), 118–32.

17. Matthew Arnold, "Rugby Chapel," in *Poetical Works of Matthew Arnold* (1890; reprint, London: Macmillan & Co., 1923), 307.

18. Cruse, *Victorians*, 263, and CH, 97.

19. Cruse, *Victorians*, 265.

20. Heilman, "New Gothic," 119.

21. Sandra M. Gilbert and Susan Gubar, eds., *The Norton Anthology of Literature by Women* (New York and London: W. W. Norton & Co., 1985), xxix.

22. Ibid.

23. See for example David Lodge, "Fire and Eyre: Charlotte Brontë's War of Earthly Elements," in *Language of Fiction: Essays in Criticism and Verbal Analysis of the English Novel* (London: Routledge & Kegan Paul, 1966), 114–43.

24. See for example John Maynard, *Charlotte Brontë and Sexuality* (Cambridge: Cambridge University Press, 1984); Jeannette King, *Jane Eyre*, Open Guides to Literature (Milton Keynes and Philadelphia: Open University Press, 1986).

25. Mary Jacobus, "The Buried Letter: Feminism and Romanticism in 'Villette,'" in *Women Writing and Writing About Women*, ed. Mary Jacobus (London: Croom Helm, 1979), 43.

26. See Wise and Symington, *The Brontës*, 3:11.

27. Shorter, *Life and Letters*, 1:10.

28. See Shorter, *Life and Letters*, 1:18–20, where he says he wished to correct omissions in Gaskell's *Life*.

29. Thomas Wise and John Symington, eds., *The Shakespeare Head Brontë*, 19 vols. (Oxford: Shakespeare Head Press, 1931–38).

30. See Fannie Ratchford, *The Brontës' Web of Childhood* (New York: Columbia University Press, 1941); Laura J. Hinkley, *The Brontës: Charlotte and Emily* (New York: Hastings House, 1945); Tom Winnifrith, *The Brontës and Their Background: Romance and Reality* (London: Macmillan, 1973).

Notes and References

31. E. F. Benson, *Charlotte Brontë* (London: Longmans, Green & Co., 1932).

32. H. E. Wroot, *The Persons and Places of the Brontë Novels* (New York: Burt Franklin, 1970), first published in 1906 by the *Brontë Society Transactions.*

33. Mrs. Ellis H. Chadwick, *In the Footsteps of the Brontës* (London: Sir Isaac Pitman & Sons, 1914).

34. Lord David Cecil, "Charlotte Brontë," in *Early Victorian Novelists* (London: Constable & Co., 1934), 112.

35. Peters, *Unquiet Soul*, 414.

36. Helene Moglen, *Charlotte Brontë: The Self Conceived* (New York: W. W. Norton & Co. 1976) and Annette Tromly, *The Cover of the Mask: The Autobiographers in Charlotte Brontë's Fiction*, English Literary Studies no. 26, (Victoria: University of Victoria Press, 1982).

37. Peters, *Unquiet Soul*, 413.

38. Cecil, *Victorian Novelists*, 112.

39. Margaret Blöm, *Charlotte Brontë*, Twayne's English Authors Series, 203 (Boston: Twayne, 1977), 13.

40. Peters, *Unquiet Soul*, 414

41. Ibid.

42. Charles Burkhart, *Charlotte Brontë: A Psychosexual Study of Her Novels* (London: Victor Gollancz, 1973), 12.

43. Robert Keefe, *Charlotte Brontë's World of Death* (Austin: University of Texas Press, 1979), xi.

44. John Maynard, *Charlotte Brontë and Sexuality* (Cambridge: Cambridge University Press, 1984), 33.

45. Maynard, *Sexuality*, ix, 39, where he says the work "should be read as an independent vision."

46. Gilbert, Sandra M., and Gubar, Susan, *The Madwoman in the Attic: The Woman Writer and the Nineteenth-Century Literary Imagination* (New Haven and London: Yale University Press, 1979), 369.

47. King, *Jane Eyre*, 75, 73.

48. Terry Eagleton, *Myths of Power: A Marxist Study of the Brontës* (London: The Macmillan Press Ltd., 1975), 13.

49. Jacobus, "Buried Letter," 42.

50. Ibid., 58.

51. Heilman, "New Gothic," 119.

52. Jacobus, "Buried Letter," 42.

53. Cecil, *Victorian Novelists*, 112.

54. Wise and Symington, *The Brontës*, 2:243.

55. Quoted in Peters, *Unquiet Soul*, 35, from Fannie E. Ratchford and William Clyde de Vane, *Legends of Angria* (New Haven: Yale University Press, 1933), xxviii.

56. Charlotte Brontë, *Shirley*, ed. Andrew and Judith Hook (1849, reprint, Harmondsworth: Penguin, 1974), 78.

57. Fannie E. Ratchford, *The Brontës' Web of Childhood* (New York: Russell & Russell, 1964), 109.

58. *Letters of William and Dorothy Wordsworth: The Middle Years*, ed. E. de Selincourt (Oxford: Oxford University Press, 1973), 2:705.

59. Shorter, *Life and Letters*, 1:387.

60. Shorter, *Life and Letters*, 2:127–28.

61. Wise and Symington, *The Brontës*, 2:209.

62. Robert Browning, *The Poetical Works*, ed. Ian Jack (London: Oxford University Press, 1970), 571.

63. The writings of Jacques Lacan are notoriously difficult; for an excellent account see Terry Eagleton, *Literary Theory: An Introduction* (Minneapolis: University of Minnesota Press, 1983), 168–71.

64. Sigmund Freud, "The Uncanny," in vol. 17 of *The Standard Edition of the Complete Psychological Works of Sigmund Freud*, trans. James Strachey (London: Hogarth Press, 1917–19), 236.

65. Ibid.

66. *Letters of Mrs. Gaskell*, ed. J. A. V. Chapple and Arthur Pollard (Manchester: Manchester University Press, 1966), 249.

67. *The Miscellaneous and Unpublished Writings of Charlotte and Patrick Brontë*, vol. 1 of *The Shakespeare Head Brontë*, ed. T. J. Wise and J. A. Symington (Oxford: Shakespeare Head Press, 1931–38) 1:7.

68. Ratchford, *Brontës' Web*, 109.

69. Wise and Symington, *The Brontës*, 2:255.

70. Ibid., 179.

71. *Jane Austen's Letters to Her Sister Cassandra and Others*, ed. R. W. Chapman (London: Oxford University Press, 1952), 468–69.

72. M. H. Abrams, *The Mirror and the Lamp: Romantic Theory and the Critical Tradition* (New York: Oxford University Press, 1953), viii.

73. See Robert Gittings, *John Keats*, 2d ed. (Harmondsworth: Pelican Books, 1972), 232; quoted from Hyder E. Rollins, ed., *The Letters of John Keats*, 2 vols. (1958) 1:203.

74. Gilbert and Gubar, *Madwoman*, 360.

75. Ratchford, *Brontës' Web*, 109.

76. Brontë, *Shirley*, 78.

77. See p. 59, and CH, 287.

78. Phyllis Chesler, *Women and Madness* (New York: Avon Books, 1972), 16.

79. See Nina Auerback, *Woman and the Demon: The Life of a Victorian Myth* (Cambridge, Mass.: Harvard University Press, 1982).

80. Shorter, *Life and Letters,* 1:139.

81. George Eliot, *Middlemarch,* ed. W. J. Harvey (1811–12; reprint, Harmondsworth: Penguin Books, 1965), 122.

82. Harold Bloom, *The Anxiety of Influence: A Theory of Poetry* (New York: Oxford University Press, 1973).

BIBLIOGRAPHY

This is a selective bibliography; only the most significant or interesting sources are listed:

Primary Sources

Individual Works

Currer Bell [pseud.]. *Jane Eyre, An Autobiography.* Edited by Currer Bell. 3 vols. London: Smith, Elder & Co., 1847.

Jane Eyre. Edited by Q. D. Leavis. Harmondsworth: Penguin Books, 1985.

Shirley: A Tale. 3 vols. London: Smith, Elder & Co., 1849.

Villette. 3 vols. London: Smith, Elder & Co., 1853.

The Professor, A Tale. 2 vols. London: Smith, Elder & Co., 1857.

Juvenilia

Five Novelettes. Edited by Winifred Gérin. London: Folio Press, 1971.

Legends of Angria. Edited by Fannie E. Ratchford and William Clyde De Vane. New Haven: Yale University Press, 1933.

The Twelve Adventurers and Other Stories. Edited by C. K. Shorter (and C. W. Hatfield). London: Hodder & Stoughton, 1925.

Bibliography

Unfinished

"Emma: A Fragment by Currer Bell" with "The Last Sketch," by William Makepeace Thackeray. *Cornhill Magazine* 1 (1866):485–98. Reprinted in *Bronte Society Transactions* 2 (1899):84–101.

Collected Editions

The Shakespeare Head Brontë. Edited by T. J. Wise and J. A. Symington. 19 vols. Oxford: Shakespeare Head Press, 1931–38. Includes novels, life and letters, poems, miscellaneous and unpublished writings.

Letters

Shorter, Clement, ed. *The Brontës: Life and Letters*. 2 vols. London: Hodder & Stoughton, 1908; New York: Haskell House (1908) 1969.

Wise, Thomas, and Symington, John, eds. *The Brontës: Their Lives, Friendships and Correspondences*. 4 vols. Oxford: Shakespeare Head Press, 1932. Reprint (4 vols. in 2). Oxford: Basil Blackwell, 1980.

Secondary Sources

Bibliographies

Christian, Mildred. "The Brontës." In *Victorian Fiction: A Guide to Research*, edited by Lionel Stevenson. New York: Modern Language Association of America, 1964. A survey of Brontë criticism up to 1964.

Passel, Anne. "Charlotte Brontë: A Bibliography of the Criticism of Her Novels." *Bulletin of Bibliography and Magazine Notes* 26 (October-December 1969):118–20; 27 (January-March 1970):13–20.

Biographies

Gaskell, Elizabeth. *The Life of Charlotte Brontë*. Edited by Alan Shelston. Harmondsworth: Penguin Books, (1975) 1981. (1st ed. London: Smith,

Elder & Co., 1857). The first, most influential, and very readable biography. Probably determined the course of subsequent Brontë criticism.

Gérin, Winifred. *Charlotte Brontë: The Evolution of Genius.* Oxford: Clarendon Press, 1967. Includes Charlotte Brontë's letters to M. Heger, donated to British Museum in 1913, calling them "the greatest single contribution to our knowledge of Charlotte Brontë."

Peters, Margot. *Unquiet Soul: A Biography of Charlotte Brontë.* New York: Doubleday & Co., 1975. A feminist analysis of Charlotte Brontë's life and art as a protest against limitations imposed on women. Sees life and art as interchangeable, often indistinguishable.

Books

Allott, Miriam, ed. *The Brontës: The Critical Heritage.* London and Boston: Routledge & Kegan Paul, 1974. Excellent survey of critical reception given to the novels by contemporaries.

———. *Casebook Series: Charlotte Brontë: "Jane Eyre" and "Villette": A Selection of Critical Essays.* London: Macmillan Press, 1973. Includes essays on *Jane Eyre* by M. H. Scargill, Kathleen Tillotson, Robert Heilman, David Compton, and David Cecil.

Blöm, Margaret. *Charlotte Brontë.* Twayne's English Authors Series, 203. Boston: Twayne, 1977. A good basic introduction to Charlotte Brontë's works, with an autobiographical bias. Useful critical bibliography.

Burkhart, Charles. *Charlotte Brontë: A Psychosexual Study of Her Novels.* London: Victor Gollancz, 1973. Reads the novels as stages in Charlotte Brontë's psychological development from "Rites of Passage" (*The Professor*) to "The Art of the Adult" (*Villette*). *Jane Eyre* is "The Art of the Adolescent." Full of generalizations. Useful critical bibliography.

Duthie, Enid. *The Foreign Vision of Charlotte Brontë.* London: Macmillan & Co., 1975. The influence of "the Brussels period" and of M. Heger on Charlotte Brontë's development as a writer. Importance of her French essays and Heger's comments on them.

Eagleton, Terry. *Myths of Power: A Marxist Study of the Brontës.* London: The Macmillan Press Ltd., 1975. Reads Charlotte Brontë's novels as myths that blend "blunt bourgeois rationality" with "flamboyant Romanticism," embodying the "structure of convergence and antagonism" between the industrial and landed ruling class. An original, brilliant study.

Hardy, Barbara. *"Jane Eyre" (Charlotte Brontë): Notes on English Literature.* New York: Barnes & Noble, 1964. A basic but interesting introduction; good analysis of symbolism, especially "Bessie's Ballad," and "Rochester's Love-Song."

Bibliography

Keefe, Robert. *Charlotte Brontë's World of Death*. Austin: University of Texas Press, 1979. Sees *Jane Eyre* as working out "the complex problem of survival," the guilt of outliving her mother and siblings. The most important event in her life was the death of her mother, causing fear of "Abandonment" to be "the central motif in all her fiction."

King, Jeannette. *Jane Eyre*. Open Guides to Literature, Milton Keynes and Philadelphia: Open University Press, 1986. The most recent, and by far the best, introduction to the novel. A close reading of the text that raises many issues of contemporary critical debate, offering new insights into both the novel and the literary criticism of this century. Intended to provide areas for discussion and analysis rather than a conclusive interpretation.

Knies, Earl A. *The Art of Charlotte Brontë*. Athens: Ohio University Press, 1969. Examines the narrative point of view in Charlotte Brontë's novels, to show how personal autobiographical elements are transformed into art.

Linder, Cynthia A. *Romantic Imagery in the Novels of Charlotte Brontë*. New York: Harper & Row, 1978. (London: Macmillan, 1978). Traces patterns of imagery in novels to see whether the "objective correlatives" are adequate for the emotion conveyed, claiming that *Jane Eyre* is part of the romantic tradition of nature as a visible manifestation of the inward state.

Lloyd Evans, Barbara, and Lloyd Evans, Gareth. *The Scribner Companion to the Brontës*. New York: Charles Scribner's Sons, 1982. (Published in Great Britain by J. M. Dent & Sons, as *Everyman's Companion to the Brontës*). Four sections on the family; the juvenilia; the published works; and the places. The commentary on *Jane Eyre* confuses Jane with Charlotte Brontë. Includes an amusing glossary of such useful words from the novels as "loike" and "mither," and a list of characters, reminding us that, for example, Lord Edward Vere was "the young buck" with whom Georgiana planned to elope!

Maynard, John. *Charlotte Brontë and Sexuality*. Cambridge: Cambridge University Press, 1984. Analyzes Charlotte Brontë's creation of a "discourse on sexuality," claiming that she "offers the fullest and most sophisticated discussion of sexual issues of any major Victorian novelist before Hardy." Not a quarry for hidden psychological meanings but an examination of Brontë's account of sexual awakening in *Jane Eyre* and the other novels. Fascinating introductory chapters on the milieu and criticism of *Jane Eyre*.

Moglen, Helene. *Charlotte Brontë: The Self Conceived*. New York: W. W. Norton & Co.; Toronto: George McCleod, 1976. Concerned with Brontë's private myth of love and the "psychosexual" aspect of relationships. Sees as "critical," the manner in which Brontë transmuted life into fiction.

O'Neill, Judith, ed. *Critics on Charlotte and Emily Brontë*. Readings in Literary Criticism Series. London: George Allen & Unwin, 1968. Essays on *Jane Eyre* by David Cecil, Kathleen Tillotson, and Robert Heilman. Also short extracts from contemporary reviews.

Tromly, Annette. *The Cover of the Mask: The Autobiographers in Charlotte Brontë's Fiction*. English Literary Studies Monograph Series No. 26. Victoria: University of Victoria Press, 1982. Examines Brontë's use of autobiography as framework by which to explore the process of self-portraiture; analyzes how the fictional autobiography enables the narrators to create their "own mythologies about themselves."

Chapters or Essays in Other Books

Cecil, Lord David. "Charlotte Brontë." In *Early Victorian Novelists*, 109–44. London: Constable & Co., 1934. Thinly disguised subjective and sexist criticism of the type Charlotte Brontë feared. Sees Charlotte Brontë's "final limitation" as the fact that "the world she created is the world of her own inner life; she is her own subject." Despite its claim that Charlotte Brontë's excellence was accidental, it has surprisingly been a much anthologized essay.

Gilbert, Sandra M., and Gubar, Susan. "A Dialogue of Self and Soul: Plain Jane's Progress." In *The Madwoman in the Attic: The Woman Writer and the Nineteenth Century Literary Imagination*, 336–71. New Haven and London: Yale University Press, 1979. Examines the "dis-eased" texts of nineteenth century women writers who both inherited and revised the patriarchal image of a creative woman as a monster: by creating mad and violent doubles the authors enact their own raging desires to escape from male houses and male text: both thematically and linguistically these women writers sought to subvert patriarchal structures. *Jane Eyre*, like Brontë's other novels, acts out "the passionate drive toward freedom which offended agents of the status quo," but it is "unable to define the full meaning of achieved freedom."

Heilman, Robert D. "Charlotte Brontë's 'New' Gothic." In *From Jane Austen to Joseph Conrad*, edited by Robert C. Rathburn and Martin Steinmann, Jr., 118–32. Minneapolis: University of Minnesota Press, 1958. Excellent article, claiming that Brontë revises and revitalizes the Gothic mode by introducing the symbolic, which "demands a more complicated response" than straight horror. In employing Gothic, Brontë is "plumbing the psyche, not inventing a weird decor."

Jacobus, Mary. "The Buried Letter: Feminism and Romanticism in 'Villette.' " In *Women Writing and Writing about Women*, edited by Mary Jacobus, 42–60. London: Croom Helm, 1979. Although not on *Jane Eyre*, is so provocative that it illuminates all of Charlotte Brontë's work, as a text "formally fissured by its own repressions" in which "doubleness informs the novel as a whole, making it secretive, unstable, and subversive."

Rich, Adrienne. "Jane Eyre: The Temptations of a Motherless Woman." In *On Lies, Secrets and Silence,* 89ff. New York: W. W. Norton & Co., 1979. Whenever Jane, who is economically powerless and motherless, undergoes certain traditional female temptations, she is also offered the alternative of a nurturing or principled woman on whom she can model herself.

Articles

Langford, Thomas. "The Three Pictures of 'Jane Eyre.' " *Victorian Newsletter* 31 (Spring 1967):47–48. Maintains that the three landscape paintings correspond to three stages of Jane's life.

Millgate, Jane. "Narrative Distance in 'Jane Eyre': The Relevance of the Pictures." *Modern Language Review* 63 (April 1968):315–19. The paintings provide clues to the "emotional colouration" of episodes, and by revealing the limited perception of the young Jane, they assist in the dual perspective of narrator/protagonist.

Moser, Lawrence. "From Portrait to Person: A Note on the Surrealistic in 'Jane Eyre.' " *Nineteenth Century Fiction* 20 (December 1965):275–81. Brontë anticipates surrealistic art in her descriptions of her landscape paintings.

INDEX

(abbreviations: CB: Charlotte Brontë; *JE: Jane Eyre.*)

Index

Coleridge, Samuel Taylor, 5
"conscientious study of Art," 24, 25,
    29, 30, 31; *see also* artistic
    dilemma dramatized
criticism of *JE*, biographical, 16–17;
    Burkhart, Charles, 18, 126;
    Cecil, Lord David, 17, 19, 128;
    Eagleton, Terry, 18, 126;
    feminist, 17–19; Gilbert and
    Gubar, 18, 128; Heilman,
    Robert, 19, 128; Jacobos,
    Mary, 18–19, 128; Keefe,
    Robert, 18, 127; King,
    Jeannette, 18, 127; Marxist,
    18; Maynard, John, 18, 127;
    Moglen, Helen, 17, 127; Peters,
    Margot, 17, 126; psychological,
    18; textual, 18; Tromly,
    Annette, 17, 128; twentieth-
    century, 17–19; *see also*
    Victorian reactions to *JE*

Darwin, Charles, 4
Diana and Mary, 35, 92–93, 94, 96
doubles as portraits of Jane, 27, 28,
    30; as Adèle, 79; as "arch-
    baiter," 69; in ballads, 35–36,
    90; in Bewick's *History of
    British Birds*, 36, 38, 69; as her
    doll, 35; as Blanche Ingram, 65;
    in her landscapes, 55–58; as
    Bertha Mason, 81–85, 90–91,
    97, 106; in mirror, 37–39, 76,
    81–82, 84; as Grace Poole, 69,
    79–81; as Rochester, 58–61,
    65–67, 106; as St John, 95–97;
    as Thornfield Manor, 105–6
dreams and unreality, 30, 55, 58,
    65–67, 67–69, 76–77, 81–84,
    103, 104

Eagleton, Terry, 18, 126
Eliot, George, 5, 99
Eliot, T. S., 44
Eyre, Jane, "anxiety of influence,"
    110; compared to "Fra Lippo
    Lippi," 34; as governess, 2; as
    "Liar," 50–51; no literary
    ancestors, 4; love of literature,

35–37; as writer, 9, 30, *32–33,
    40–42, 54–55, 59–61, 107–10,
    116–17*; *see also* artistic
    development, Jane's; doubles as
    portraits of Jane; journey as
    metaphor; paintings and
    drawings, Jane's; place as
    metaphor; religious belief,
    Jane's
Eyre, John, as implied author, 99–
    100

fictional autobiography, most
    important aspect of *JE*, 24; *see
    also* artistic development,
    Jane's; artistic dilemma
    dramatized; self-reflexivity of
    JE
French review of *JE*, 14
Freud, Sigmund, 38, 56, 57–58

Gaskell, Elizabeth, 3, 24, 54–55;
    author of *The Life of Charlotte
    Brontë* (1857), 14–16, 125–26
"Genius of the Storm," the, 57–58
Gilbert, Sandra, and Susan Gubar,
    8, 18, 128
Gothic, 5, 6, 56, 106
governess, CB on, 2, 80

Heilman, Robert, 6, 8, 19, 128

imagination, CB's conception of,
    fear of, 4, 25–26, 83, 85; as
    open country, 29, 60–61; as
    "Genius of the Storm," 57–58;
    as Bertha Mason, 82–83, 85; as
    "master," 60–61, 72, 79, 91,
    109–10; new confidence in,
    108; her salvation, 27; as
    "sculptor," 28, 58–59, 83;
    visual, 24–29, 108; *see also*
    artistic dilemma dramatized;
    journey as metaphor; Mason,
    Bertha; place as metaphor;
    Rochester
Ingram, Blanche, 63–65; as Jane's
    double, 65

Jane Eyre

ABOUT THE AUTHOR

Maggie Berg received her D.Phil. from Oxford University in 1978 and went to Dalhousie University, Nova Scotia, the following year on a Killam Post-Doctoral Fellowship. She subsequently taught at the University of British Columbia and McGill University, specializing in Victorian literature, critical theory, and women's writing. She was then a visiting professor at the University of Toulouse, teaching among other things a graduate course in l'écriture feminine. She has published articles on the Pre-Raphaelites and on John Ruskin, and is currently working on a book on hysteria and postmodernism in Victorian women's fiction.